Lisbon
— What the Tourist Should See —

The Pessoa Edition from Shearsman Books:

Selected English Poems

Collected Poems of Alberto Caeiro
(translated by Chris Daniels)

Collected Poems of Álvaro de Campos Vol. 1 (1916–1927)
Collected Poems of Álvaro de Campos Vol. 2 (1928–1935)
(translated by Chris Daniels)

Message / Mensagem
(bilingual edition; translated by Jonathan Griffin)
(co-publication with The Menard Press)

Zbigniew Kotowicz: *Fernando Pessoa – Voices of a Nomadic Soul*
(co-publication with The Menard Press)

Fernando Pessoa

Lisbon
—What the Tourist Should See—

Shearsman Books
Exeter

First published in in the United Kingdom in 2008 by
Shearsman Books Ltd
58 Velwell Road
Exeter EX4 4LD

www.shearsman.com

ISBN 978-1-905700-75-2

The maps in this volume are all reproduced from Karl Baedeker's *Espagne et Portugal* (Leipzig: Karl Baedeker, Éditeur, 1920). The photographs are all taken from period postcards in the collection of Tony Frazer.

Contents

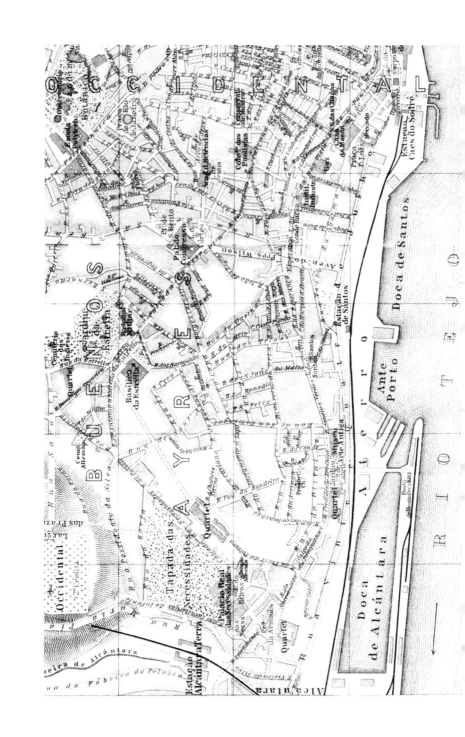

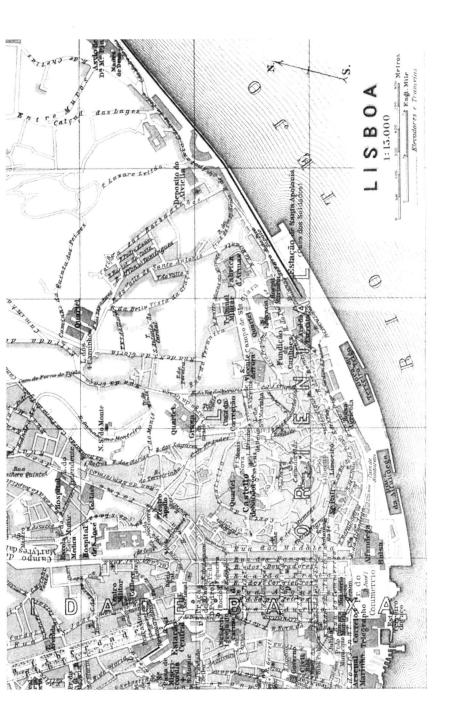

LISBOA

1:15.000

Elevadores e Tramvias

Introduction

Fernando Pessoa wrote this guide to Lisbon, in English, at some point during the 1920s. It was never published and the manuscript was only found amongst his papers long after his death. Its interest is twofold: anything from Pessoa's pen is *de facto* of interest, but he is also the quintessential city poet, and very much the poet of the city of Lisbon. He loved the city, knew all its corners, and scarcely left it after his early years there, following his school-days in Durban. The book can still be used as a guide today. The text has been updated only so as to take account of the modern Portuguese spelling of names and places. Despite the fact that more than eighty years have elapsed since the manuscript was written, the book can still be used by tourists in Lisbon as a guide, but it is, above all, useful for fans of Pessoa's own work—and their numbers continue to grow. With very good reason.

The maps in this volume are taken from the 1920 French edition of the Baedeker guide to Spain and Portugal. The photographs are all from pre-war postcards, dating from roughly 1920 up until the late 1930s.

Tony Frazer
May 2008

Panoramic view of Lisbon, ca. 1935

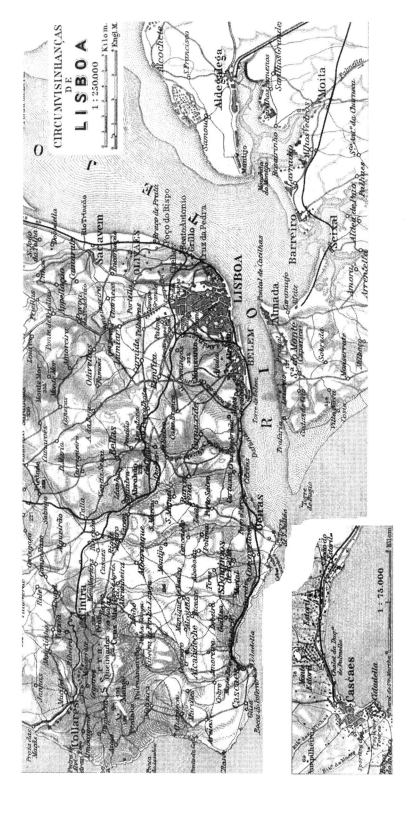

Over seven hills, which are as many points of observation whence the most magnificent panoramas may be enjoyed, the vast irregular and many-coloured mass of houses that constitute Lisbon is scattered.

For the traveller who comes in from the sea, Lisbon, even from afar, rises like a fair vision in a dream, clear-cut against a bright blue sky which the sun gladdens with its gold. And the domes, the monuments, the old castles jut up above the mass of houses, like far-off heralds of this delightful seat, of this blessed region.

The tourist's wonder begins when the ship approaches the bar, and, after passing the *Bugio* lighthouse—that little guardian-tower at the mouth of the river, built three centuries ago on the plan of Friar João Turriano—the castled *Tower of Belém* appears, a magnificent specimen of sixteenth century military architecture, in the romanic-gothic-moorish style (*see photo on page 61*). As the ship moves forward, the river grows more narrow, soon to widen again, forming one of the largest natural harbours in the world, with ample anchorage for the greatest of fleets. Then, on the left, the masses of houses cluster brightly over the hills. That is *Lisbon*.

Landing is easy and quick enough; it is effected at a point of the bank where means of transport abound. A carriage, a motor-car, or even a common electric tram, will carry the stranger in a few minutes right to the centre of the city. On the wharf every facility awaits him, for the officials he finds there are invariably polite and ready to give him every indication he may require, whether he address the customs officials or those of the port or immigration police.

Outside the Customs building there is a small police station which comes in very useful, as it controls the porterage of luggage, to avoid the abuses which, but for that, would be inevitable anywhere in such circumstances. This station sends luggage to any part of the city and takes upon itself the responsibility for the delivery. The officials are fully competent and speak several languages.

We shall now ask the tourist to come with us. We will act as his cicerone and go over the capital with him, pointing out to him the monuments, the gardens, the more remarkable buildings, the museums—all that is in

Rocha do Conde de Óbidos

Escadinhas da Rocha do Conde d'Obidos e Doca.

Stairway from the Rocha do Conde de Óbidos, & docks

any way worth seeing in this marvellous Lisbon. After his luggage has been handed to a trustworthy porter, who will deliver it at the hotel if the tourist is staying awhile, let him take his place with us in a motor-car and go on towards the centre of the city. On the way we will be showing him everything that is worth seeing.

Right in front of the wharf he has just left is the *Rocha do Conde de Óbidos*, an eminence crowned with a well kept garden which is reached by two large stone stairways; from the garden itself, at the top, there is a fine view over the river. Going along the *Rua 24 de Julho*, we pass the Santos Gardens (or Vasco da Gama Gardens) and soon afterwards the Gardens of *Praça de Dom Luís*, where there is the bronze statue of one of the heroic commanders of the liberal campaigns, the Marquis de Sá da Bandeira; the monument itself, sculptured by Giovanni Ciniselli, was cast in Rome, and the base made in Lisbon by Germano José de Salles and erected in 1881.

A little further on, and after passing the fine building where the services of the National Aid to Consumptives (Assistência Nacional aos Tuberculosos), founded by Queen Amelia, are installed, let us notice this square that stretches right up to the river; on the left there is a monument to the *Duke da Terceira*, who freed Lisbon from the absolutist government, and on the right a small but interesting marble statue figuring a sailor at the helm. This monument is due to the sculptor Francisco dos Santos, the Duke's to the sculptor Simões de Almeida. Near by are the provisional railway station of the Cascais line, and on the river the quay for the small steamers which cross the Tagus. There is also a motor-car stand here.

Our car moves on, goes through the Rua do Arsenal, and passes the Town Hall *(Câmara Municipal)*, one of the finest buildings in the city. It is remarkable both outside and inside and is due to the architect Domingos Parente, the collaboration of celebrated artists being noticeable in the stone, in the paintings, etc. The monumental staircase which leads to the first floor is worth seeing, especially on account of the magnificent paintings which decorate the walls and the ceiling; and the several rooms of the building are no less nobly decorated with frescoes and canvases by Sequeira, Columbano, José Rodrigues, Neves Júnior, Malhoa, Salgado, etc., representing historical and other figures, with a great picture by Lupi representing the Marquis de Pombal and the reconstruction of Lisbon effected by him after the great earthquake, as well as with busts by the foremost sculptors, artistic fireplaces, furniture, etc.

In the middle of the square we shall see the Pillory *(Pelourinho)*, very well-known abroad; it is a masterpiece of the late eighteenth century, a spiral made out of a single stone. On the right side of this square, as we pass it, we shall note the Naval Arsenal *(Arsenal da Marinha)*, a vast building containing, besides the arsenal and the workshops—which, with the docks, are on the river and therefore invisible to us—, the Naval College *(Escola Naval)*, established in 1845, and the Court of Appeal *(Tribunal da Relação),* in the halls of which some fine specimens of old tapestry may be admired. Other public offices, of lesser note, are also installed in this building. Further on, in a different but not separate part of the building, facing the side of the Town Hall, are the Post and Telegraph Offices, though only the entrance to the Poste Restante part of the former is on this side.

We now reach the largest of Lisbon squares, the *Praça do Commercio,* formerly *Terreiro do Paço,* as it is still commonly known; this is the square which is known to Englishmen as Black Horse Square and is one of the largest in the world. It is a vast space, perfectly square, lined on

Lisboa. Praca Do Commercio.

three sides by buildings of a uniform type, with high stone arches. All the chief public offices are installed here—the Ministries (except that of Foreign Affairs), the Postal and Telegraphic Offices, the Customs House, the Attorney General of the Republic, the Emigration Office, the Administrative Court, the central office of the Red Cross, etc. The fourth, or South, side of the square is formed by the Tagus itself, very wide in this part and always full of shipping. In the centre of the square stands the bronze *equestrian statue* of King José I, a splendid sculpture by Joaquim Machado de Castro, cast in Portugal, in a single piece, in 1774. It is 14 metres high. The pedestal is adorned with magnificent figures depicting the rebuilding of Lisbon after the great earthquake in 1755. There is a figure guiding a horse which treads the enemy under its hoofs, another with the palm of Victory, Fame in another group; and the aggregate is remarkable indeed. Besides this, we can see there the Royal Arms and the portrait of the Marquis de Pombal, as also an allegory figuring Royal Generosity rebuilding Lisbon from its ruins. High railings, joined to columns, surround the monument, and marble steps lead up to it.

On the North side of the square, facing the river, there are three parallel streets; the middle one issues from a magnificent triumphal arch of great dimensions, indubitably one of the largest ones in Europe. It is dated 1873, but it was designed by Verissimo José da Costa and began to be built in 1755. The allegoric group which crowns the arch, sculptured by Calmels, personifies Glory crowning Genius and Valour; and the recumbent figures, which represent the rivers Tagus and Douro, as well as the statues of Nuno Álvares, Viriato, Pombal and Vasco da Gama, are due to the sculptor Victor Bastos.

The Terreiro do Paço is one of the places where boats are taken to cross the river; on the right-hand side, facing the river and on it, is the provisional station of the Southern Railways. It also often happens that tourists land here, as commonly do the crews of foreign men-of-war which visit the port. There is also a carriage and motor-car stand in this square.

The general aspect of the square is of a kind to give a very agreeable impression to the most exacting of tourists.

From the Praça do Commercio we can go on to the centre of city by any of the three streets which go North from there Rua do Ouro on the left, Rua Augusta (the one with the arch) in the middle, and Rua da Prata on the right. Let us choose Rua do Ouro, which, owing to its commercial importance, is the main street of the city. There are several banks, restaurants, and shops of all kinds in this street; many of the shops, especially towards the upper end of the artery, will be found to be as luxurious as their Parisian equivalents.

Almost at the upper end of the street, on the left-hand side as we go up, there is the *Santa Justa Elevator,* so called because the transversal street in which it is built is called Rua de Santa Justa. This is one of the "sights" of Lisbon and always compels great admiration from tourists from everywhere. It is due to a French engineer, Raoul Mesnier, to whom other interesting projects are also due. The elevator is all built in iron, but it is extremely distinctive, light and safe. There are two lifts, worked by electricity. It goes up to Largo do Carmo, where there are the ruins of Carmo Church, now the Archaeological Museum. Authority is needed to go right up to the top, above where the lifts themselves stop; from there a magnificent panorama is got of the whole city and the river. The elevator belongs to the Electric Tramway Company.

We have now reached *Praça D. Pedro IV,* commonly known as *Rocio* or *Rossio.* This is a vast quadrangular space lined on all sides except the North one by buildings of the Pombal type; it is the chief Lisbon centre, almost all lines of transport passing there. In the middle of the square stands the statue of D. Pedro IV, which dates from 1870; it was designed by Davioud and sculptured by Elias Robert.

This monument is one of the highest in Lisbon, being over 27 metres high. It comprises a stone base, a marble pedestal, a column of white marble, and a bronze statue. The lower part contains four allegorical figures, representing Justice, Strength, Prudence and Temperance, as well as the shields of sixteen of the chief Portuguese towns. North and South of this monument there are two ponds with bronze fountains, surrounded by flower-plots.

On the North side of the square stands the *Teatro Nacional Almeida Garrett,* which dates from 1846, and is due to the Italian architect Fortunato Lodi. The front of this building is remarkable; it includes six monumental columns which were formerly part of the Church of S. Francisco da Cidade. The statue of Gil Vicente and those of Thalia and Melpomene are by Assis Rodrigues, on sketches by António Manuel da Fonseca; the figures representing Apollo and the Muses by the same artist; while other figures, representing certain dramatists, and the reliefs figuring the four phases of the day, were sketched by Fonseca and worked by Assis Rodrigues. All these render the building very interesting. It is no less interesting inside, the theatre itself being a fine one, with a ceiling painted by Columbano. The hall is also very fine.

It was almost on this very spot that the old Inquisition stood.

The great movement and traffic to be seen in the Rossio is due to the fact that the greater part of the tramway lines pass through the square, to the great number of shops, hotels and cafés which the square contains, and also to the proximity of the Lisbon Central Railway Station, of the Portuguese Railway Company (Companhia dos Caminhos de Ferro Portugueses).

The station building faces the western side of the theatre. The front is in "Manueline" style, profusely

dentelée, with great windowed doors of horse-shoe shape.
The clock at top is an electrical one, and connected with
those inside the station. On the ground floor are the ticket-
offices for the general lines, an information bureau and
a luggage clearance office. There is a lift for those who
do not wish to go up the stairway to the top floor, which
is in level with the railway lines themselves, a perplexing
circumstance for those who forget the hilly character of
the city. On this top floor we find the ticket-offices for the
suburban lines, a police station, the station-ticket office, a
hand-luggage depot and another depot for the clearance
of heavier luggage. Several doors give admittance to the
station properly such. This top floor or pavement of the
station is also reached by an incline going up from two
points in Rua Primeiro de Dezembro; this is the approach
chosen by carriages and motor-cars, which thus go right
up into the covered space which leads into the top floor.
Within this covered space there is a postal and telegraphic
office which is open up to the departure of the last mail-
trains.

The building of this Railway Station, which was designed by the architect José Luís Monteiro, was begun in 1887 and completed three years afterwards, the official opening taking place on the 11th June, 1890.

We are now therefore right in the middle of Lisbon. The tourist, whether he has come by sea, or has stepped out here from the railway station, is now in the right place to choose his hotel, should he not be leaving that very day. As a matter of fact the chief hotels are situated in Rossio itself, or very near it.

Once he has booked his rooms, the tourist will naturally walk out to see the city. Two steps outside Rossio, going East, he will find the *Praça da Figueira;* this is the central Lisbon market, and is built on a site formerly occupied by All Saints Hospital, by the Convent of St. Camillo and by other buildings. This market is very popular and lively; it is built in iron with a glass roof, and is made up of a large number of small shops and stalls, facing the streets and the inside of the building. The best time to see it is in the morning, when it offers an animated scene.

Let us, however, take up our course from the point we had arrived at—the Central Railway Station. Going further up, we enter the great Avenida da Liberdade, or, to be more precise, the *Praça dos Restauradores,* which is the beginning of it. In the middle of this "square" we shall find the monument which commemorates the Campaigns of Restoration, which date from 1640 onwards. The monument, with base, pedestal and obelisk, is 30 metres high and is due to a design by António Thomas da Fonseca. On its lower part are two figures symbolizing the geniuses of Victory and of Liberty, the former by Simões de Almeida and the latter by Alberto Nunes; the monument also bears the dates of the chief battles in the campaigns which followed the Revolution of 1640. This obelisk was erected in 1886. In this "square" there are carriage, motor-car and motor-cycle with side-car stands.

A little higher up, at the corner of Calçada da Gloria, there is the large building called *Palacio Foz;* it is in this building that the Club dos Restauradores (Maxim)—see p. 70—is installed.

The *Avenida da Liberdade* (i.e., Liberty Avenue), opened in 1882, is the finest artery in Lisbon. It is 90 metres wide and 1500 metres long, full of trees from beginning to end, and includes small gardens, ponds, fountains, cascades and statues. It goes up in imperceptible incline and offers a magnificent perspective. This great improvement in Lisbon is due to Rosa Araújo, who was then president of the Town Council.

Right at the beginning of the Avenida we find two marble ponds, one on either side of the mainway; further up there are, in the same manner, two fine cascades, girt round by luxuriant vegetation, the waters of which come from two figures representing the rivers Douro and Tagus. A little higher up, on the right, we see a small but interesting monument to *Pinheiro Chagas,* an author and journalist; the monument represents him and also the heroine of one of his dramatic works. This monument was erected by the initiative of the weekly *Mala da Europa* in 1908.

On the left-hand side, at the place where Rua do Salitre begins, the first stone was placed on the 9th April 1923 for the monument to be erected to the memory of these fallen in the Great War. In front of this place, on the same side, is the Club Avenida Palace, and, at the back of this, with entrance by Travessa do Salitre, the Avenida Parque, where there are theatres and other popular amusements.

The garden plots which follow on up the Avenida are closed by four marble statues representing Europe, Africa, Asia and Oceania. In the Avenida da Liberdade there are two theatres, four cinemas, and several cafés and confectioners; it contains also some palatial residences. During the summer months, some of the cafés spread their service up into the central garden-plots, which are profusely lit; this open-air service, with the music added to it, enlivens the whole Avenida on summer evenings.

The Avenida ends in what is called the Rotunda, or, officially, *Praça Marquês de Pombal*. This is the site chosen for the erection of the monument to this great Portuguese statesman. The first stone for this monument was laid on the 8th May 1882—the centenary of the Marquis's death—by King Luís; the monument itself, which is in process of erection, is designed by the architect Adães Bermudes and by António Couto, the sculpture work by Francisco dos Santos. It will be 36 metres high, commanding five large avenues which meet at that spot. The foundations rest on a rocky basis at a depth of 18 metres. The monument, according to the project, will represent the great statesman, on his pedestal of glory, contemplating his formidable work—the reconstruction of Lisbon after the great earthquake, the substitution of slavery by Work and Study—, and will also show the chief collaborators of the Marquis in this great achievement: José de Seabra, Dom Luís da Cunha, Conde de Lippe, Luís António Verney, Dr. Ribeiro Sanches, Manuel da Maya, Eugénio dos Santos and Machado de Castro. There will also be seen numerous inscriptions describing the chief acts of the great reformer. The base of the monument will be of granite, the bowls and columns in coloured marble and gilt bronze, the statues and bas-reliefs in cast bronze, the statue of Lisbon in white marble, as also the trophies, the eagles and the support of the terminal group; the inscriptions will be in gilt bronze and in cast bronze the group which completes the monument itself.

From this spot great avenues stretch out towards the more modern quarters of the city. It was here that, from the early morning of the 3rd to that of the 5th October 1910, those troops encamped which, under the command of Admiral Machado Santos, overthrew the Monarchy and proclaimed the Republic.

One of the avenues which starts from the Praça Marques de Pombal is the Avenida Fontes Pereira de Mello, where there are fine private houses and palatial residences, the chief one being that of the millionaire Sotto Mayor; a little further up, at the corner of Avenida 5 de Outubro and Rua Pinheiro Chagas, there is the house of Malhoa, the painter, designed by the architect Norte Júnior.

This avenue ends in *Praça Duque de Saldanha*, which contains the monument of the great liberal Marshal who gives the square its name; this monument, designed by Tomás Costa and Ventura Terra, was unveiled in 1909. The base of the monument contains a bronze figure of Victory.

Going now up the Avenida da Republica, which is well paved and full of trees, and where also some interesting private residences are to be seen, we shall notice, on the right-hand side the large and bold *Praça de Touros do Campo Pequeno* (Campo Pequeno Bull-fight Ring—*see photo, next page*), dating from 1892, and built in brick in the Moorish style on the design by the architect António José Dias da Silva. The Ring has an area of 5,000 square metres and holds 8,500 people.

Let us go on further, through the tunnel under the railway line; we come to another monument in course of construction. The site is at the end of this Avenue, and the monument is meant to commemorate the Peninsular War, which in 1808 freed Portugal from foreign domination, and in which so many Portuguese displayed remarkable

heroism. This monument will be one of the finest in the country. The first stone was laid in 1908, on the occasion of the first centenary of the popular rising; and the monument was adjudicated in competition to José and Francisco de Oliveira Ferreira, two brothers, the first a sculptor and the second an architect, who sent in a project remarkable for nobility and beauty. The monument will be about 16 metres high. The work of the two Portuguese artists represents Portugal as a castle; a pantheon of men who won renown, a coffer of relics that the people heroically defends. It alludes to the discoveries of Gama and Cabral, and markedly defines, in its aggregate, the patriotic sentiment that inspired it. In its lower part there are several groups of figures that symbolize: in front, the people in revolt, in fierce defence of its past glories; on the left, the effort and turmoil of war; on the back, a lion, popular strength, resting on the debris of combat; on the right, the ruins of humble dwellings, a sacked church, and a girl kneeling by her father, both weeping the ill fate that has come upon them. The tombs of Portuguese ancestors are also seen. The aggregate is crowned by an allegoric

24

group—the Portuguese wresting their flag from the claws of the imperial eagle, to give it back to their own victorious country.

All the lower groups, and the pedestal, will be of white marble from Pero Pinheiro, and the chief group of bronze, cast in the Army Arsenal. All the sculpture work was executed by Jose de Oliveira Ferreira in his studio at Praia de Miramar.

We now enter one of the finest parks in the city—the *Campo Grande*, over a kilometre in length and about 200 metres broad throughout. This was a field for military manoeuvres a good while ago, and it was Queen Maria I who ordered the first plantations to be made there. We find there valuable specimens of exotic trees, ornamental plants, flowers, etc. There is a pond for pleasure boating, a buffet installed in a little island in the middle of this pond, a skating rink, a tennis court, swings for children, thatched arbours, band stands, bicycles for hire, and so on. On the left, in front of this pond, which is commonly called Lago dos Barcos (Boat Lagoon — *see photo below*), there is the

Lago do Campo Grande.

Jockey Club Hippodrome, a vast space admirably adapted to the purpose which its name described, as also for races of other sorts. The course is 1500 metres long and it is 30

metres wide in its diameter from the starting point; there are three stands or tribunes, one for the President of the Republic, and two others, in reinforced concrete, being one for the members of the Jockey Club and another for the general public. The latter accommodates 6000 persons. The general standing space provides accommodation for nearly 60,000, and there is a buffet and the due space for the racehorses. The *pari mutuel,* on the French system, is already instituted.

Contiguous to this field there will eventually be a Stadium, of the size of the Stockholm one, for the training of athletes for the Olympic Games, as also for football matches, a polo ground and golf-links.

The Jockey Club, which was established in July 1925, owes its inception to the public-spirited initiative of a number of Lisbon sportsmen, who are thereby worthy of all praise.

A few steps further on, the *Chalet das Canas* (Cane Chalet) is worth seeing; it is built entirely of all sorts of canes and tree-trunks, is adorned with oil-paintings, and contains hothouse plants, an aquarium and an adjoining garden with exotic plants of great botanic value. This chalet was built under the supervision of a former administrator of the park gardens, António Cordeiro Feio.

The Campo Grande park is one of the most popular Sunday resorts; the crowd scatters itself throughout the several lanes which have been artistically cut in the park, and it is frequent to see lively courses of riders and carriages in the left-hand side road. At the bottom of the Campo there is the football ground belonging to the Sporting Club de Portugal, and, as we go round and back, we shall see on our left the Dom Pedro V Poor-House, the Bordalo Pinheiro Museum, which is very curious, and the bronze monument to this famous national draughtsman, a sculpture by Raul Xavier.

Our motor-car now comes back again through the Avenida da Republica, crosses rapidly the Estefânia Quarter, where the hospital of the same name is situated, and, traversing Avenida Almirante Reis, goes up to *Senhora do Monte,* a hill from the top of which one of the finest views of all Lisbon is to be had, either at night, or at sunrise or sunset. We are now on the way to Monte da Graça, where one of the best Lisbon churches is situated; this is the church where may be seen the famous image of *Senhor dos Passos* (made of Brazil wood and articulated) which used to figure in the annual procession, named after the image, which was suspended on the establishment of the Republic. From the stone yard of this church a magnificent panorama of the city and river may also be enjoyed, almost as fine as the one from Senhora do Monte.

Going down Rua da Voz do Operario, our car now stops in front of another majestic temple—the Church of *São Vicente de Fora*—where there is much to admire. The front in seventeenth century Renaissance style, is simply magnificent, with its niches with images of St. Anthony, St. Dominic, St. Sebastian, St. Austin, St. Vincent, St. Norbert and S. Bruno. An ample stairway leads up to the church itself.

This grandiose temple was built in 1147 by Afonso Henriques, the first king of Portugal, and rebuilt in 1627 on a design by the architect Filipe Tersi. If the church is remarkable on the outside, it is no less remarkable within. It is 74 metres long and 18 wide, with fine lateral chapels, the best of which is that of Senhora da Conceição, all in marble, with inlaid work; a high-altar due to the collaboration of two great artists, Venegas and Machado de Castro; a magnificent choir, with a sumptuous organ; remarkable canvases in the nave and the vestry, which is superbly adorned; cloisters full of fine glazed-tile pictures; and the convent entry with paintings by V. Baccarelli, restored by Manuel da Costa, etc. From the terrace of this church a very good view of the Tagus may be had.

In what was formerly the convent refectory the *Royal Pantheon of the House of Braganza* is now installed; the adaptation was made by order of King Fernando II, in 1855. The first to enter be buried here was King João IV, one year afterwards.

The entry is by the right-hand door in the front of the church, the door which gives admittance to the cloisters of the old palace of the Patriarch of Lisbon. On the right are the administrative offices of the 1st and 2nd quarters of the city, and on the left, following the long corridor, there is, halfway down it, the old vestry made by order of King João V, all in inlaid marble. Almost in front there is a stone stairway which leads to the São Vicente Lyceum (High-School). Right at the end a large mahogany door gives ingress to the Pantheon itself. At the entrance to the corridor, which is 17 metres long and 4½ wide, there are two tombs in the wall; two heroes rest there—the Duke de Saldanha and the Duke da Terceira and the tombs are a fitting homage to the battles which they won. In front of the latter lies his wife, who had the same title. .

The Pantheon is 36 metres long and 9 wide; there are two lateral raised parts on which are placed the coffins and urns with the mortal remains of kings and princes. On the right lies King João IV, founder of the Braganza dynasty, which began with the Revolution of 1640, prepared by forty noblemen, led by the great patriot João Pinto Ribeiro.

In the middle lies Dom Pedro IV, who was King of Portugal and Emperor of Brazil; there are two crowns on the urn, representing the two countries over which he reigned. This king was distinguished in the war against his brother Dom Miguel, and stood for constitutional government against the absolutism of the latter.

Next lies Prince Afonso, brother of King Carlos, in a sumptuous silver coffin weighing over six hundred kilos. In front of Dom Afonso lies King Carlos, whom two murderous bullets killed on the 1st of February, 1908, when, returning from Villa Viçosa, he was crossing the Praça do Commercio in an open carriage. During his reign Portugal obtained several brilliant victories in Africa—those of Mouzinho de Albuquerque over the rebel chief Gungunhana in Mozambique, and those of Major Roçadas over the Cuamata tribe in Angola.

A little further on lies King Carlos' son, Dom Luís Filipe, who was assassinated on the same occasion.

On the sides are several important figures of the Portuguese Royal Family, among which Kings Luís I and Fernando II, who, like Dom Carlos and his son, are in urns with crystal tops. Dom Fernando is least altered, though he has lain there for forty years.

The Pantheon, which is visited every year by more than twenty thousand persons, is in the keeping of the Central Committee for the Execution of the Disestablishment Law; this Committee deserves all praise for the care it has taken of the royal vault. The Pantheon may be visited on all weekdays, from 10 a.m. to 5 p.m.; one escudo, which reverts to charity, is all that there is to pay.

Going on from Largo de São Vicente, taking to the left and passing under the lateral arch, we reach a vast space, the *Campo de Santa Clara,* where on all Tuesdays and Saturdays may be observed the Feira da Ladra, a picturesque market of odds and ends, some useful, some rather doubtfully so, some new, some old, but all of them no doubt quite a profitable business for the strange sellers that on those days stretch their wares along the pavements in the open air. Sometimes, indeed, quite valuable curios, both artistic and archaeological, turn up here. Further on in this square there is little garden, on the left of which stands the Military Court. Going down, on the right, there is a building which, had it ever been finished, would have been one of the finest religious monuments of the seventeenth century; this is the *Church of Santa Engrácia,* all in masonry, with marvellously worked marble. It was once thought of adapting this building to a National Pantheon, but the project has as yet gone no further. Even in its incomplete state, this church is worth seeing. It is at present serving as an army depot.

Going further down, we see, a little way below, the Arms Factory (Fabrica de Armas), which adjoins the Army Arsenal. The Navy Hospital is there also, dating from the eighteenth century.

We now enter Rua do Mirante, turn at Rua Diogo do Couto, and come out at Bica do Sapato. On the left are Poço do Bispo, Xabregas, and other populous and industrial quarters. On the way we may admire the *Church of Madre de Deus,* the convent of which was founded in 1509 by Queen Leonor. It is an abundantly restored structure, but still full of noble and artistic details in inlaid work and painting, especially in the vestry and the choir.

Towards the right we now find ourselves in the square named after the Artillery Museum (Museu de Artilharia); this square contains the Santa Apolónia Railway Station, which is the Lisbon goods station. In front of this stands the Army Arsenal (Arsenal do Exército), and it is in this building that the *Artillery Museum* is installed. This museum is indubitably the most remarkable one in Lisbon. It was founded in 1842 by Baron de Monte Pedral, but it was only in 1876 that it became really a grand museum, owing to the efforts of its director, Captain Eduardo Ernesto de Castelbranco. This museum contains several things well worth seeing—a fine collection of ordnance and other arms, cuirasses, weapons, as also the decorations of the halls themselves, in inlaid work, panelling, portraits, busts, statues, medallions and bas-reliefs; uniforms dating from the time of the Peninsular War, etc. The collection of ordnance (nearly 300 units), which figured in the Portuguese campaigns in Europe, in Africa and in the East, is magnificent; they are real living relics of a glorious past. The paintings, signed by masters like Columbano, Malhoa, Velloso Salgado, Carlos Reis, Ramalho, Luciano Freire, Condeixa, Jorge Collaço, João Vaz, Acácio Lino, Sousa Lopes, Falcão Trigoso, etc.; the sculptures, by Simões de Almeida (the nephew), Oliveira Ferreira, Sousa Rodrigues and others; the gilt inlaid-work and other decorative elements—all these render this museum a remarkable storehouse of masterpieces, which no visitor to Lisbon should miss seeing.

The Artillery Museum is installed, as we have said, in the *Army Arsenal* building, which dates from the eighteenth century and possesses, turned towards the railway station side, a monumental entrance with an admirable allegoric group due to the sculptor Teixeira Lopes. The Museum is open on all weekdays, except Mondays, from 11 a.m. to 5 p.m.

On our way back to the *Baixa,* that is to say, the central and low part of the city, we pass by one of the most picturesque quarters of Lisbon—*Alfama,* the old fishermen's quarter, which still retains a great part of its ancient aspect. The tourist who can spend a few days in Lisbon should not omit to visit this quarter; he will get a notion no other place can give him of what Lisbon was like in the past. Everything will evoke that past here—the architecture, the type of streets, the arches and stairways, the wooden balconies, the very habits of the people who live there a life full of noise, of talk, of songs, of poverty and of dirt.

After passing by the Cais da Fundição, which is the wharf which serves the vessels which go to and come from Africa, we enter the Rua da Alfândega. On the right, at the very beginning, is the Travessa dos Bicos. The tourist gets out of his car and goes to see the *Casa dos Bicos* (Pointed House). This building dates from the sixteenth century and belonged to the descendants of the great Afonso de Albuquerque. The front is all in pointed stones, and for this reason they used to call it Casa dos Diamantes (Diamond House). It is an architectural curiosity well worth looking at.

We get back into our car. A little further on, in the same street we are now going through, is the church called *Conceição Velha,* which is worth our attention; the porch is in Manueline style, with delicate stone-work, and we see there, in semi-relief, the figures of Senhora da Misericordia (Our Lady of Mercy), King Manuel I and Dona Leonor his Queen, founders of the Misericordia, Pope Leo X, and several saints, bishops, etc. This church was built in 1520, and, having suffered from earthquakes, was rebuilt after the last great one, in 1755. The temple is also worth seeing inside, though not especially remarkable in that respect.

A few yards further is Rua da Magdalena. Our car goes up this and turns to the right, on the way to the *Se Patriarcal,* the Lisbon Cathedral; this temple is extremely old, the date of its erection being unknown, though it is believed that it dates from far before the Moorish dominion, and at most due to King Afonso Henriques. The several earthquakes from which Lisbon has suffered left their traces on this temple, which has been several times restored; but it must be said it has been very badly restored, since its present state shows the lack of a definite plan on the part of the several "restorers". It is at present in course of a more vigilant restoration, supervised by

António Couto, and it is hoped that the reconstruction will put some artistic unity into the cathedral.

This temple was the scene of several facts which made history, as, for instance, of the popular rising in 1383, during which Bishop Dom Martinho Annes was thrown from one of the towers, owing to his partiality to the policy of Dona Leonor Telles.

On the inside, the Sé is worth a careful visit, which should not miss its three naves, the arches, the stained-glass windows, the baptismal font where it is supposed that Saint Anthony was baptized in 1195, the chapel of Bartolomeu Joanes, the Machado de Castro stall, and the several paintings which may there be seen. There are also the tombs of the founder of the chapel just mentioned, of archbishops Dom Rodrigo da Cunha and Dom Miguel de Castro, of King Afonso IV and of his Queen, daughter of Sancho IV, of Castile, of Lopo Fernandes Pacheco and his second wife Maria Rodrigues. From the top of the choir and from the galleries nearly the whole church can be seen.

The cathedral contains a perfect treasure of ritual objects of all sorts, in gold, silver and precious stones, of very considerable value. One of the most remarkable elements of that treasure is the famous *Custodia da Sé,* which is 90 centimetres high and is gold all through, with diamonds, emeralds, rubies and other precious stones, in an astonishing total of 4120. The four-faced base weighs 75 marks, that is to say, 17,212 kilogrammes. It was made by a celebrated artist, José Caetano de Carvalho, who spent five and half years over it, and had the honour to present it to King José I in 1760, the king making a gift of it to his royal chapel. The work itself cost 18 contos (£4,000). Another equally remarkable treasure is the so-called *Philippine Cross,* in many-coloured enamel, given by

Philip II of Spain to the Convent of Christ, in Tomar, in 1619. The museum formed by all those treasures is not, however, open to the general public.

A little further up, in what was formerly the palace of the archbishop Dom Miguel de Castro, is the female gaol called *Aljube*. It has no claim on our attention except that of the historic past of the building itself. On the opposite side of the street, that is, on the right as we go up, there is the other gaol, *Limoeiro,* for male prisoners. This big building was built, as it now is, in the eighteenth century, but the site is closely linked with the past history of Portugal. The Paço dos Infantes (i.e., Princes' Palace) was once here, and it was there that Conde de Andeiro, lover of Queen Dona Leonor, was killed by the Master of Avis; King Fernando died there; there were once the Mint, the Town Council House, the old Court of Appeal, etc. The Limoeiro is the oldest of civil gaols in Lisbon; it was converted into a gaol in the 18th century. A few years ago some of the prisoners set fire to it and part was burnt; this part has not yet been rebuilt.

Almost in front of the Limoeiro is the Rua da Saudade, which leads to *Castelo de São Jorge* (St. George's Castle). The tourist who has time to spare should not miss going up to this castle which is built on an eminence which commands a view of the Tagus and of a great part of the city. The castle has three chief doors, known as Treason, Martim Moniz and São Jorge doors. The three are very ancient. The castle itself is remarkable enough. It was built by the Moors and formed, so it seems, part of the defences of Lisbon, with its thick walls, its battlements and its towers. There did kings dwell; and it was the scene of many a remarkable event in the political history of Portugal. Nowadays, though surrounded and choked by a great number of houses, full of barracks, modified, spoilt and mutilated by earthquakes and misuse, it is still worth seeing for what it once was. The view from the castle is marvellous. It may be visited by requesting permission to so from the day-officer of the barracks.

After visiting the Castle of St. George, or having seen the Limoeiro, let us go down again to Rossio, where we may admire the magnificent and vast Church of *São Domingos* (St. Dominic), in the side-square of the same denomination; this church was built after the great earthquake, and is due to the architect Mardel. The more important official ceremonials were carried out there—royal marriages and christenings, coronations, funeral services. King Carlos was married there. The high chapel, in dark marble, with medallions on the base, is well worth seeing, as are also the tombs of Prince Afonso, son of King Afonso III, and of Friar João de Vasconcellos, and the paintings, by Pedro Alexandrino, which adorn the several chapels.

In this same spot stood once the church of the Convent of São Domingos, destroyed by the 1755 earthquake, where the Inquisition effected many of its *autos da fé*. It was also in this church that, in 1506, after divine service, many Jews were killed by the fanatical populace, the massacre spreading soon to other parts of the city.

Going from here along Rua Eugénio dos Santos, we shall see, facing Rua do Jardim do Regedor, the Monumental Club, and a little further on, also on our right, the palatial building where the Sociedade de Geografia (Geographical Society) is installed since 1897. This Society was founded in 1875 by Luciano Cordeiro, and has played a highly patriotic role, promoting lectures, congresses, exhibitions, national commemorations, scientific expeditions, etc. We find there an interesting colonial and ethnographical museum, which comprises naval relics, models of galleons and national and African boats, busts and other sculptures, armour, arrows and other native weapons, flags and banners of military expeditions, oil paintings by famous lands, manuscripts, engravings, Indian furniture, historic furniture, wild animal skins, specimens of fibre textiles and of such like stuffs, products of Angola, Mozambique, Macau, Timor, etc., such as coffee, rubber, timber, and so on, native idols, teeth of animals, skulls, birds, models of the typical costumes of the Portuguese provinces, globes, sarcophagi, and a thousand other curious things which fill the vestibule, the staircases of the three floors, three large and four smaller rooms, and two orders of galleries which go round the Sala Portugal (Portugal Hall), which is the largest of all, having an area of 790 square metres. This museum is open to the public on Sundays, from 11 a.m. to 4 p.m., but with special authority it may be visited on weekdays.

The same large building contains the Coliseu dos Recreios, one of the largest theatres and circuses in all Europe. Almost in front of it is the Associação Commercial de Lisboa (Lisbon Chamber of Commerce) in a building of its own, formerly the property of the Palace Club.

Our car now crosses Rossio again, goes up Rua do Carmo, Rua Garrett (better known as *Chiado*), and turning at Rua Ivens, stops at the end of this, in the square which contains the old Convento de São Francisco da Cidade, founded in 1217, where the National Library, the Art School and the Museum of Contemporary Art are now installed, as also the Governo Civil, which, however, has its front in Rua Capello.

The *Escola de Bellas Artes* (Art School), on the first floor, was opened in 1837, and its teaching covers drawing, painting, sculpture, engraving, architecture, etc. Some artists—Columbano, Carlos Reis, Salgado and Luciano Freire—have their studios there.

The *National Museum of Contemporary Art* contains fine paintings and sculptures dating from 1850 onwards. There are canvases by Cristiano da Silva, Bordalo Pinheiro, Miguel Ângelo Lupi, Tomás J. da Annunciação, Alfredo de Andrade, Visconde de Menezes, António Manuel da Fonseca, José Rodrigues, Francisco Metrass, Assis Rodrigues, Victor Bastos, Simões de Almeida, Alfredo Keil, Moreira Rato, Silva Porto, Bonnat, António Ramalho, Alberto Besnard, Sousa Pinto, Angel, José Malhoa, Paul Laurens, Condeixa, Carlos Reis, Trigoso, Salgado, João Vaz, Artur Loureiro, Muñoz Degrain, Sousa Lopes, Constantino Fernandes, etc.; sculptures by Costa Motta, Francisco Santos, Teixeira Lopes, Simões Sobrinho, Moreira Rato, Soares dos Reis, Alberto Nunes, Tomás Costa, Anjos Teixeira; drawings by Lupi, António Carneiro, Ramalho, Silva Porto, Bordalo Pinheiro, Sousa Pinto, Victor Bastos, Sousa Lopes, etc.; water-colours by Alves de Sá, Roque Gameiro, Alberto de Sousa, Helena Gameiro, Leitão de Barros, Carlos Bonvalot, etc. There is, in fine, much to see and to admire in this museum, which is fitly installed.

The National Library *(Biblioteca Nacional)* is on the second floor. It was founded in 1796 with the name of *Real Biblioteca Pública da Corte* (Royal Court Public Library), being made up with the books that formed the library of the Board of Censors, that is to say, the books that had belonged to the Jesuits and to the Royal Academy of History. The library has been successively added to by purchase and gift. The library has 11 rooms and 14 passages, on two floors, and contains 360,000 volumes. At the entrance stands the statue of Queen Maria I, by Machado de Castro, and the busts of Castilho (by Jose Simões de Almeida) and of Dom António da Costa. The coloured glazed-tiles *(azulejos)* of the sixteenth century are worth seeing; they formerly belonged to the Senhora da Vida chapel, in St. Andrew's Church, now no longer in existence.

On the lower of the two floors are the reading-rooms for private investigation and public reading, the catalogue room and the newspaper and review room. On the upper floor are the printing office, the offices, the engraving department, and the very important Reserved Book room, which contains the rarer works, real bibliographic relics, some unique copies, specimens of rare binding and illustration, manuscripts, coins, and many written documents of all kinds, all the which form a bibliographic collection worthy of the greatest possible care. And it is but just to say that this department of the Library, as indeed all the others, do receive now proper care and vigilance. The Bibliotheca is now remarkable for its cleanness and good installation, especially considering that the building is not of the fittest for the purpose. Recently, and especially since Dr. Jaime Cortesão, a well-known poet and author, was appointed Chief Librarian, the Library has made a marked, and very needed, progress.

The visitor may also see the special Bible Department (which possesses one of the two extant copies of the first edition of the Mainz or Gutenberg Bible), the Navy and Overseas Archives, which include maps and charts, the cataloguing room, the Library of the Convent of Varatojo, which maintains its original setting, including the oratory, the Fialho de Almeida Room, with this writer's bust (by Costa Motta, the nephew), etc.

There is a vast terrace on the top of the building, with a very fine view. The Library is open on, all weekdays from 11 a.m. to 5 p.m. and from 7.30 to 10 p.m.

Turning down Rua Capello, which leaves the middle of Rua Ivens, we find the Governo Civil (corresponding to the French "Prefecture"). This building contains the

General Command and several sections of the Police, and, on the first floor, the Passport Office.

A little further on, in the Largo do Directório, stands the *Teatro de São Carlos* (St. Charles' Theatre), built in 1792, in homage to Princess Carlota Joaquina de Bourbon, by the initiative of several Lisbon merchants and capitalists, the architect being José da Costa e Silva. The work began on the 8th December of that year, and six months afterwards the theatre was finished; it was opened on the 30th June 1793 with Cimarosa's opera *La Ballerina Amante.*

This theatre is a first-class one, and the greatest vocal celebrities in the world have been heard there, as, for example, Tamagno, Gayarre, Patti, Battistini, Bonci, Barrientos, Caruso, Tita Rufo, Regina Paccini, Francisco and Antonio de Andrade, etc. It has seen conductors like Saint-Saëns, Toscanini, Mascagni, Strauss, Liszt, Mancinelli, Leoncavallo, Victorino Guy, Tullio Serafin, etc. The building itself is an interesting one, with a terrace over the archways which form the covered entrance to the theatre. The vestibule, the ceiling of which was once one painted by Cirilo Wolkmar Machado, is now limited to stucco with arms, decorations, and several panels with dates of when celebrated operas were first heard here, marble columns, and kindred ornaments of great artistic effect.

The theatre proper, oval in shape, is very majestic and well-designed; the decoration, wholly in gilding, is by Manuel da Costa; and the acoustic conditions of the room are unexceptional. There are five orders of boxes, large galleries and an ample pit, accommodating 600 persons without any sacrifice of comfort. A huge chandelier, 10.9 metres in circumference and bearing 284 lamps, hangs from the centre of the ceiling. On the second floor there is also a large and nobly decorated hall.

The Teatro de São Carlos, which cost 166 contos (£36,880) and was built on the lines of the Naples theatre of the same name which was burnt down on the 13th February 1816, is since 1854 the property of the State. It is a pity that at present it should be occupied by dramatic, instead of opera, companies.

Let us now enter Rua Garrett and go up to the Largo das Duas Egrejas. On left stands the monument to Poeta Chiado (i.e., the Poet Chiado), the name popularly given to a sixteenth century friar, António do Espírito Santo, who abandoned his habit to become a sort of embodiment of the rollicking spirit of the times and to develop into the favourite popular poet; his extant poems show considerable merit. This statue is due to the sculptor Costa Motta (the elder); it was erected by order of the Town Council and unveiled on the 18th December 1925.

We now enter *Praça Luís de Camões,* in the middle of which stands the monument to the great epic poet, a work of the sculptor Victor Bastos, unveiled in 1867. The statue is in bronze, and the pedestal shows the stone statues of Fernão Lopes the historian, Gomes Eannes de Azurara the chronicle-writer, Pedro Nunes the cosmographist, Fernão Lopes de Castanheda and João de Barros the historians, and of Jerónimo Corte-Real, Vasco Mouzinho de Quevedo and Francisco de Sá de Menezes, poets all three. The monument is 11 metres high and the open space in which it stands is girt round with trees, where a legion of feathered visitors does duty for the leaves in winter.

Going a little down Rua do Alecrim, we find, in the Largo do Barão de Quintella, the statue of the novelist *Eça de Queiroz,* by Teixeira Lopes, unveiled in 1903. The chief figure, in marble, represents Truth—a naked woman whose body is imperfectly veiled by a gauze covering.

Above and behind it is the 'novelist's bust. On the base is graven a phrase of the great author's which was the sculptor's inspiration—"On the strong nakedness of truth the transparent veil of fancy".

Let us now turn back and return to Rua Garrett; a little off it, going up on the left, is the Largo do Carmo, where once stood the *Convento do Carmo,* a monastery founded in 1389 by the great constable Dom Nuno Álvares Pereira, in fulfilment of a vow made at the battle of Aljubarrota. The founder professed, died and was buried there; he was afterwards transferred to the Egreja de São Vicente, where the body remained for many years. In March 1918 he was taken to the Monastery of Jerónimos, whence again he was transferred to the little church of the Third Order of Carmelites, where he now is.

The church of the Convento do Carmo was a remarkable one. It had three majestically impressive naves, which were partly destroyed by the great earthquake.

More than half of what was the convent building is now occupied by the central barracks of the Republican Guard. The old church and some adjacent parts to-day compose the *Museu Arqueológico* (Archaeological Museum), where there are tombs, statues, inscriptions, heraldic and otherwise, earthenware, coins, etc. Special attention should be given to the fourteenth century baptismal font, where the sons of King João I were baptized, the Moorish basin from the Penha Longa convent, a stone basin brought from Azamor, a marble statue of Queen Maria I, executed in Rome by José António de Aguiar for a monument that was never erected, the stone cross of São Lázaro, the tombs of Rui de Menezes, Dona Isabel de Lima, Gonçalo de Sousa and São Frei Gil, a window from the Jerónimos, a statue of St. John Nepomuceno, King Fernando's tomb, sixteenth century glazed-tiles (*azulejos*) from the convents of Chelas and of Santo Eloy, a model in wood of the Constable's tomb, which the great earthquake destroyed, as also many of the coins, medals and other objects, among which two mummies figure. The chief entrance, formed by a doorway with six ogive arches, is one of the finest of its time. The Archaeological Association is at present installed here. The museum itself is open to the public on all days except Mondays, from 11 a.m. to 5.30 p.m. The admittance is only one escudo.

Our car now goes on to the Church of São Roque, in Largo Trindade Coelho. This church dates back to the later years of the sixteenth century, Filipe Terzi being the architect; it was rebuilt after the Great Earthquake. The inside of the temple is interesting especially owing to the wooden ceiling, painted in 1588, the mosaic decorations in marble, many-coloured glazed tiles and gilt inlaid work, fine paintings by Bento Coelho da Silveira, Gaspar Dias, Vieira Lusitano and others and several tombs, among which those of Dom António de Castro, son of Dom João de Castro (1632), Dr. Francisco Suarez (1617), Dom Tomás de Almeida, first patriarch of Lisbon, and Father Simão Rodrigues (1579), who instituted in Portugal the Society of Jesus.

But the important—nay, the unique—point about this church is the *Chapel of St. John the Baptist (Capella de São João Baptista)*, which was executed in Rome by order of King João V, blessed there by Pope Benedict XIV in 1744, and fitted up in the church in 1749. It is remarkable not only for its material value but for its artistic one, for there is perhaps nowhere else anything of the kind which can bear comparison with it. The architectural work is due to the celebrated Italian architect Salvi e Vanvitelli, to whom are also due the finest works of the kind in his own country. To the execution of this work the best artists of the time, in sculpture, mosaic, metalwork and other arts were all contributors.

The chapel is a work of the highest art, abounding in all the applications of marble and bronze—the former in a marvellous range of colours, the latter in all sorts of ornaments, emblems, royal arms, monograms, and so on. The altar is an artistic marvel, in which the most varied and the finest of all Italian stones were brought into play; the result is an aggregate effect which justly perpetuates the memory of a Portuguese king who knew how to be an artist too.

Besides the arch at the entrance and the confessionals, the pictures *The Baptism of Christ, Pentecost* and *The Annunciation,* by Moretti working on Massucci's sketches, are well worth seeing; they are executed in mosaic. The side-doors and the gates are no less beautiful.

The tourist who has a sense of art should let his attention be taken by the magnificent branched candlesticks, in chased silver and bronze, masterpieces of such artists as Simone Miglie, Ricciani and Pietro Werschaffelt, as also by the composite piece on the altar, made up of six candlesticks and a cross in gilt bronze.

We turn now to the museum which adjoins the church. It is a priceless collection of furniture and ornaments which are part of the Chapel which we have just been visiting. There are thuribles, reliquaries, crucifixes, etc., in an aggregate splendour of precious-metal-work which no other country can pride itself on possessing. And the tourist must not omit to remark the two great chased silver torch-stands, the work of the famous Giuseppe Gagliardi, which have only once left the museum; they figured in the funeral service of Dr. Sidónio Pais, the ill-fated President of the Republic, who was assassinated on the upper floor of Rossio Railway Station, on the night of the 14th December 1918, as he was going to take the Northern express. Each torch-stand weighs about 380 kilogrammes and is 2,85 metres high.

The Chapel of St. John the Baptist cost £ 225,000 in good gold coinage, an extraordinary sum at any time, and more so at the time it was built.

The museum is open to the public on the last Sunday of each month, but it can be visited on any day by obtaining authority therefor at the Church. There is a descriptive catalogue of the Chapel by Souza Viterbo and R. Vicente de Almeida.

We get out and turn to the right, and a little further on we find São Pedro de Alcântara (*see photo opposite*), an esplanade from which one of the finest views of a great part of the city can be obtained. From here may be seen the several hills of the eastern side of Lisbon—Castello, Graça, Senhora do Monte, Penha de França—a good deal of the lower city, and, beyond that, the broad, calm river right away to Barreiro, Alcochete, etc., on the South bank. At night the panorama is no less remarkable. On leaving this esplanade, which is full of trees, and contains a little monument to a journalist, Eduardo Coelho, and going down a stone stairway, we find ourselves on what may be called a lower floor of the esplanade—a fine garden with exotic trees, statues, ponds, and a public library. It is an ideal place for rest and meditation.

Going up Rua D. Pedro Quinto, we soon see another garden, in Praça Rio de Janeiro; it is one of the finest gardens in Lisbon owing to its careful plan and to the care given to it. This garden contains some fine specimens of trees, the most remarkable one being a spreading cedar, the branches of which, resting on iron-work, cover ground enough to hold some hundreds of persons. Under this fine cedar-tree another public library is installed; it is one of the six which the Town Council, owing to a happy idea of one

of its members, Alexandre Ferreira, distributed among the Lisbon gardens. On the left stands the monument to França Borges, a celebrated journalist. The monument is due to the sculptor Maximiano Alves, and is composed of several superimposed blocks of rough stone, having on the right a female figure, symbolizing the Republic, that looks tenderly at the semblance of the great propagandist. This monument was unveiled on the 4th of November, 1925; since then the garden bears officially the name of the democrat whose monument is set there.

Going further on, and straight on, we see on the right the building of the Escola Polytechnica, where the Faculty of Sciences is now installed. This building was erected in 1844 on the ground belonging to the Novitiate of the Society of Jesus.

In some buildings adjoining the Escola the *Museu Bocage* (Zoological Museum) is installed. This museum is worth visiting, for it contains some curious specimens. In the Sala Portugal there are some remarkable fishes; there is a strange one, 8.4 metres long and 3.6 metres round which was caught at Paço d'Arcos by King Carlos. There is also

45

an enormous tortoise caught in the Peniche coast. After the Sala Portugal, there is the Sala de Africa Portuguesa (Portuguese Africa Room) with a very important and varied collection; the Mammals Room, with a very fair amount of specimens from all over the world; the Birds Room, the Invertebrates Room, the Skeletons Room, and such like. The number of specimens, covering mammals, birds, reptiles, fishes, etc., is over 20,000, and there are more than 50,000 insects. The shell collection, which is enormous, must also not be forgotten.

As the installation is undergoing, in so far as the building is concerned, extensive repairs, there is no definite day for visitors; but, if the due authority is requested, the place can be visited every day between 12.30 and 6.30 p.m.

This Museum is installed in the first floor of the building; on the ground floor are the Botanical Museum, and the Museum of Geology and Mineralogy. The latter is especially remarkable, one of its most interesting exhibits being a large mass of native copper, partly covered with cuprite, weighing 1224 kilos; this comes from Mamocabo stream, near the town of Cachoeira, 120 kilometres from Bahia (Brazil), and was brought to Portugal as far back as 1792.

This building has adjoining it a garden which is one of the most picturesque in Lisbon, and even in Europe; so, at least, many foreigners have said. It contains specimens of the flora of all regions of the world. The garden is in a slope, and this is one of its great points, for the incline has been put to good use to get every possible effect out of the varied vegetation that everywhere rises up, giving the aggregate an Edenic splendour. The garden contains several ponds, cascades, brooks, bridges, labyrinths, a fine hot-house, etc. In its upper part stands the Meteorological Observatory named after Infante Dom Luís, and inaugurated in 1863, and also the Astronomical Observatory.

The tourist, should he so wish it, can go right through the garden and come out at the lower door, in Praça da Alegria, going on from there to the Avenida da Liberdade; but, as we are taking another route, we shall come out again at Rua da Escola Politécnica, passing a few yards onward by the Imprensa Nacional (National Printing Office); this building has nothing at all remarkable about it, but it is large and perfectly fitted for the purpose for which it was designed. The typesetting and printing departments, as also the foundry, are well installed. All official publications are printed here. The Imprensa Nacional has made great progress these later years, owing to the very able administration of its present director. The building contains some oil-paintings which once belonged to the Casa Literária, at Arco do Cego, and a library with several thousand volumes.

We move onward and, after passing the Largo de São Mamede, and, on the right, the palace of the Dukes de Palmela, we reach the Praça do Brazil, where several tram -lines meet. From this square we go on, along Rua de São Filipe Nery, and enter Rua de Artilharia Um, on the left side of which stand the barracks which once were those of the First Artillery, after which the street is named, and are now occupied by the Republican Guard. On the right stretch the vast grounds of Parque Eduardo VII (Edward VII Park). It was on these grounds that, on the 5th December 1917, Sidónio Pais, entrenched himself, with several regiments of the Lisbon garrison, and overthrew the "democratic" government in which Norton de Mattos was Minister of War. Other revolutionary movements of minor importance have chosen this strategic point as there starting one, for it commands Lisbon and the river.

Entering now Rua Marquês da Fronteira, we pass by the old *Penitenciaria* (i.e., Gaol), which is now called Cadeia Nacional de Lisboa. This building was designed by the engineer Ricardo Júlio Ferraz, and it was begun in 1874. The front has two towers in the central part, and the building on the inside has the form of a star with several wings meeting at a central point, easy to observe. It is a large building, containing 474 cells, and a further 22 for sick-rooms, 12 punishment-cells, and 26 workshops for several crafts, the work of some of these being taken up by important firms. There is a department for the sale to the public of the products of the workshops. There is also a very curious museum, composed of the strangest and most varied weapons with which crimes have been committed, from rifles and carbines to knives of all sorts, and implements not designed for the express purpose of taking away life. The Penitenciaria may be visited on Sundays, from 9 a.m. to noon, but on other days it is not difficult to obtain permission, which must be applied for in the place itself, to visit the building.

Having got thus far, the tourist should not now omit to visit one of the finest, pleasure grounds in Lisbon—the Parque Eduardo VII, already alluded to, which stands in the vast grounds in front of the Penitenciaria. The Park hothouse is a magnificent work, of which Lisbon should be proud; and it is strange indeed that part of the population of the capital not only should not visit it, but should even ignore its very existence. Yet that almost unknown corner is a wonder of cool delight, where Nature shows us many of her choicest specimens in ornamental plants and where the art of humble artists, but with a modest genius of their own, delight our eyes with careful greenery and flowers. The hot-house contains thousands of specimens of exotic plants, the value of which it is not easy to reckon. The hothouse is open to the public on Sundays and holidays, from 8 a.m. to 7 p.m., and the admittance is one escudo. On weekdays it is open from 8 a.m. to 5 p.m. and there is no charge for admittance.

Returning to the same street and turning to the left, and going down to Campolide, we get sight of the *Aqueduto das Águas Livres*, a magnificent specimen of old engineering which is still the just object of admiration.

Lisboa.
Aqueduto das Aguas Livres.

The Aqueduct is, as a matter of fact, a gigantic work, with a total extent, in its branches, of 59,838 metres (nearly 40 miles), of which 4,650 metres are underground. There are 109 arches with 137 skylights. The most important part is the one that passes in Campolide, over the Alcântara river; it is 941 metres long and contains 35 arches, the central arch having the maximum height of 65.29 metres, and a width of 28.86 metres.

This Aqueduct, a real national monument, and perhaps the most remarkable of its kind in Europe, has always attracted a great attention from foreigners, and earned from them a consensus of praise which is altogether deserved. It was begun in 1729 and took 20 years to build. The project is due to Manuel da Maia and Custódio Vieira, and the whole work cost 13 million cruzados—nearly one and a half million pounds, a stupendous sum for the time. Transit over the aqueduct was once public, but it was closed to stop the several suicides and crimes that took place there. It may still be visited, however, by obtaining the permission of the guards. The view from there is an admirable one, as may easily be imagined.

We have seen the Aqueduct from the front. Behind it, at the end, lies the Serra de Monsanto, a hill which is crowned by a fort, which is now used as a gaol and as the chief wireless station in continental Portugal. We turn down Rua General Taborda and then down Rua Ferreira Chaves, and on our way get a side view of both the Aqueduct and the Serra.

We go up Rua Conde das Antas and down Rua das Amoreiras till we reach Rua Silva Carvalho, which is on the right. Going along this street, we come out of it at Rua da Estrella, at the beginning of which are the British Cemetery and the British Hospital. If we turn to the right, through Rua Saraiva de Carvalho and crossing Rua Ferreira Borges, we shall see at the top the German Cemetery, and further on, right at the end, the Prazeres Cemetery. If we turn to the left, at the intersection of the two streets, we shall go down to Largo da Estrella. If, however, coming back to Rua da Estrella, we go down it, we shall come to the side entrance to the *Jardim da Estrella* (Estrella Gardens), which is one of the best kept in the capital. It was opened in 1842, and has several fine specimens of exotic flora, a good number of ponds, a grotto, hothouses, an open air library, a band-stand, amusements for children, a buffet, an artificial hillock, statues, delft animals by Bordalo Pinheiro, etc. The statues are *The Digger*, by Costa Motta (the elder);

Awaking, by Simões de Almeida (the younger); *King's Daughter Keeping Ducks,* by Costa Motta (the younger); and *The Fountain,* by Maria da Gloria Ribeiro da Cruz.

Next to this garden stands the Military Hospital, which occupies a large and fine building which once belonged to the Benedictine Friars.

Facing the chief entrance to the Gardens there is the fine *Basilica da Estrella,* a majestic temple, built by the order of Queen Maria I, and dedicated to the worship of Jesus' Heart *(Corafilo de Jesus).* It was built from 1779 to 1790, the architects being Mateus Vicente and Reinaldo Manuel.

The Basilica da Estrella, the front of which, with its images in niches and large statues, is very fine, has two bell-towers of good design, with large clocks. On the top of the church there is a vast terrace, from which a wide view of the city may be obtained. But the really great view is not be had from there, but from the top of the dome, which rises at the latter end of the terrace, and to which we ascend by a stairway of 212 stone steps. From the gallery which crowns the dome almost all the modern part of Lisbon can be seen, as also the river at its greatest width and some of the more important villages on the Southern bank.

The inside of the church is also worth seeing. There are sculptures by Machado de Castro and paintings by Pompeo Batoni, representing Princess Maria Benedicta, sister of the Queen who founded the Basilica, and Princess Mariana. This church contains likewise the tomb of Queen Maria herself and a child's "mummy" brought in 1791 from the Roman catacombs, a gift from Pope Pius VI.

To the right of the Basilica lie the building containing the Head Geodesical Department and a few buildings belonging to the Military Hospital already referred to.

We shall now go down the Calçada das Necessidades and, crossing Largo do Rilvas, come to the *Palácio das Necessidades,* a large palace where Portuguese kings have dwelt and many heads of foreign states been received as guests. The building was erected in 1745, Caetano Tomás de Sousa being the architect; it was built in only five years. It was there that King Carlos, and his Queen, Dona Amelia de Orleans, used to live, and King Manuel afterwards. The greater part of the very valuable contents of the palace was sent to the Museum of Old Art and to other palaces after the advent of the Republic; but there are still many things worth seeing there—paintings, portraits, inlaid work, gold and silver work, the chapel, containing statues by Giusti and José de Almeida and rich furniture and ornaments, the magnificent gardens, and the great park full of exotic trees and shrubs, hothouses, ponds, statues, etc.

The Palácio das Necessidades is now occupied (the front part) by the Ministry of Foreign Affairs, which was transferred there after the Republic came in, and (the rear part) by the Head Barracks of the First Division, entrance to which is by Largo do Rilvas.

We shall now go down towards Alcântara, and, crossing the Railway line, up the Calçada da Tapada till we reach the gate of *Tapada da Ajuda.* Admission is 1.50 escudos for motor-cars, 1 escudo for carriages, 50 cents for motor-cycles and horses, and 30 cents for simple admission per person. At the entrance stands the bust of the agriculturist Ferreira Lapa. At the top is the building where the Higher Agricultural Institute *(Instituto Superior de Agronomia)* is installed; from there we can see the bar of the Tagus, the Necessidades Park, the Prazeres Cemetery, etc. Within the Tapada lie also the National Agricultural Museum and the Astronomical Observatory created in 1861 by King Pedro V.

We leave the Tapada by the Sitio do Casalinho gate; we go down, and then up again the *Palácio da Ajuda,* a vast building without real architectural importance, but nevertheless worth seeing. The front is very ample but very sober. The vestibule contains several small allegorical statues by Machado de Castro, Joaquim José de Barros, Amatucci, Faustino José Rodrigues, G. Viegas and José de Aguiar. The paintings are by Vieira Portuense, Domingos Sequeira and others.

Inside, the Palace is worthy of more attention. It contains very fine furniture, and excellent specimens of bronze, earthenware and other work, as also paintings and tapestry of considerable value. There are fine statues and mirrors, chandeliers, artistic clocks, carpets and curtains, and an infinity of other ornaments minor in size but not in interest. Two of the rooms are especially worth seeing—the Sala de Saxe, where walls, ceilings, furniture, and all else, show the celebrated little figures bearing that name; and the Sala de Mármore (Marble Room), where everything, walls, pavement and ceiling, is in marble.

This important building, which may be visited with due permission, was begun in 1802 and was designed by the architect Fabri. The work took a long time, and, as a matter of fact, was never really brought to an end, several alterations being introduced into the original design. Dona Isabel Maria, who was Regent of the Kingdom, dwelt there, as also Dom Miguel, who was here acclaimed absolute king. Dom Carlos, of Spain, stayed here in 1833, and when the Republic was proclaimed Queen Maria Pia and Prince Afonso were living there.

On the ground floor is the Library, founded by the Marquis de Pombal; the great historian Alexandre Herculano and the celebrated author Ramalho Ortigão were two of the more remarkable among its librarians.

The library contains about 24,000 volumes, including many historic documents, parchments, religious and diplomatic manuscripts, etc.

As we go down the Calçada da Ajuda, we see on our right the *Jardim Botânico da Ajuda,* which was organized by order of the Marquis de Pombal. It still includes trees planted in 1811. The garden is a fine one, covering three and a half hectares (about 9 acres) and is so situated that a fine view of the Tagus may be had from there. There is a tree there which is two hundred odd years old and has a trunk with a circumference of 42 metres. There are many ponds and statues, and well-kept hothouses. The garden may be visited with due permission.

Going on along Rua do Jardim Botânico, we find, in the square at the end of it, the *Igreja da Memória,* a church built by order of King Jose I in thankful "memory" of having escaped from a plot for his assassination in 1758, on this spot.

The church was designed by the architect João Carlos Bibiena, and is all on masonry and wrought marble. The high chapel contains a painting by Pedro Alexandrino which is allusive to the plot. The remains of the Marquis de Pombal were conveyed hither in 1923 from the Merces Chapel.

A few minutes more, and we are in front of the great monument that is the *Mosteiro* (Monastery) *dos Jerónimos (see photo opposite),* a masterpiece in stone, which all tourists visit and which they never can forget. It is, as a matter of fact, the most remarkable monument which the capital contains. Its construction was ordered in 1502 by King Manuel I, the architect being Boitaca, who is the author of other remarkable works of the kind in Portugal.

The side door is of an architectural richness which is the wonder and delight of all. It is an astonishing specimen

of stone-work, full of niches, of statues, of reliefs, arms and emblems, the two more prominent items being the statue of Prince Henry the Navigator, and, at the top, the image of Our Lady of Belém (i.e., Bethlehem), with a barred window beyond. The effect of this monumental door, as an aggregate, is of an exquisite harmony, deeply and softly religious, and it sets us thinking of the marvellous hands that moulded and executed it. Portugal had within itself, at that time, the greatest masters of stone-work, both national and foreign, and they have left trace of their work in masterpieces like the Jerónimos.

The western front, built in 1517, is due to the remarkable French artist, Nicolas de Chanterenne, who began Renaissance architecture in Portugal. It is a magnificent work and shows the great resources of the master who designed it. In all its details there is an exquisite perception of proportion and effect in the arches, in the frames, in the shields and emblems, in the small and large niches, peopled with statues, in all the figures and ornaments which reflect the soft mysticism of the time. Besides the two lateral niches, there are three others, set above them; these contain the statues of the Nativity, the Annunciation, and the Adoration of the Three Kings. In two other niches, King Manuel and Queen Maria, kneeling under the protection of St. John the Baptist and St. Jerome. The varied motifs of the ornaments, the placing of the statues, the framing of these—all was planned and executed by skilled and careful hands, which the centuries shall for over thank for the beauty which they wrought.

Entering the temple, we should first visit the Capela do Baptismo (Baptism Chapel), which is on the left; the urns of João de Deus and Almeida Garrett are temporarily there, and will afterwards be placed in the confessionals next to the one where the body of Sidónio Pais has been put. These confessionals are in the wall in front. At the cross, on the left, is the Almeida Garrett Chapel, where lie, in the upper part, Cardinal Dom Henrique, who was king of Portugal, and, on the sides, the nine children of King Manuel I. In the centre, on the ground, lies the first stone which was laid on the 9th December 1905 by Prince Luís Filipe, to mark the place for the tomb of Almeida Garrett, from whom the chapel henceforward takes its name. It was in this place that, on the 21st December 1918, the body of Dr. Sidónio Pais, President of the Republic, was set; the body being followed to the monastery by a crowd of many thousands, in a moving and heart-felt demonstration. The body was afterwards transferred to the Capela do Baptismo, and later on to the fourth confessional, counting from the cross, where it still remains.

On the right is the vestry, remarkable both for its architectonic beauty and for its paintings. Returning to

13. LISBOA. Jerónimos.
Tumulos de Vasco da Gama e de Luiz de Camões

*Monastery of
Jerónimos: the tombs
of Vasco da Gama
and Luís de Camões.*

57

the Church, we find the Chapel of St. Jerome, whose image, in enamelled terracotta, is due to the celebrated Luca della Robbia. It is of this image that the story is related that Philip II of Spain, on coming face to face with it and marking its wonderful expression, exclaimed «*No me hablas, Hierónimo?*» (*"Won't you speak to me, Jerome?"*).

Let us next admire the magnificent pulpit, marvellously wrought, and, next, the High Chapel, where, on the Gospel side, lie King Manuel I and his Queen Maria Fernanda. On the Epistle side lie his son, King João III, and his Queen, Catarina Filipa of Castile, whose tombs, in Estremoz marble, rest on two elephants each hewn from a sole block, and with teeth of the very first ivory that was brought from India. The tabernacle of the High Chapel, all silver-covered, was offered by Pedro II, when a prince, in 1675. Its author is Gil Vicente. Over the tabernacle there are magnificent pictures.

We continue our visit, and see in front of the Almeida Garrett Chapel the tombs of Luís de Camões and Vasco da Gama (*see photo, previous page*), made in 1894 under the guidance of the sculptor Costa Motta. In the upper part of this chapel is the tomb of King Sebastian, and at the sides those of the sons of King João III and grandsons of King Manuel I. In the niche to the left of King Sebastian's tomb there is the image of St. Gabriel, which belongs to the Chapel of Nossa Senhora do Desterro, and was taken by Vasco da Gama da India in the caravel which he commanded. The vault which rises over the cross is an admirable work, and contains the real bronze escutcheons which belonged to the caravels that went to India and to Brazil. The whole inside is wonderfully wrought, in reliefs of unparalleled beauty. The working of the columns that sustain the vault is no less remarkable. The central column of the vestry is worth looking at for a long time. Through the vestry we can go to the choir and the cloisters, where there is also much to see.

A visit to Jerónimos is bound to be a slow one, if it is to be a visit at all. All the beauties it contains must be carefully examined: the working of all details, the images, the tombs, the columns, the vaults, especially that of the transept, which no column sustains, the paintings, the choir, whence the greater part of the inside of the church may be seen, the cloister, which is one of the finest in the world, the Chapter House, with the tombs of Alexandre Herculano and of the great poet Guerra Junqueiro, the old Galilee, where the dormitories used to be, the Chapel of Christ, etc.

In the west part of the monastery the *Casa Pia* is installed; it was founded in 1780 and transferred hither

Lisboa D'o, Covro dos Jeronimos Terraeno do Claustro

in 1833. The Casa Pia derives its income from legacies and from part of the proceeds of the lottery. It maintains nearly 800 boarders, who learn several professions, and subsidizes others, already earning their life outside, but who do not yet earn enough, or those others who are at universities or technical schools. It is one of the oldest and best managed of the educational charity institutions in Lisbon.

The *Museu Etnológico (Ethnological Museum)*, installed in the last wing of the building, which is open to the public on all week-days except Mondays from 11 a.m. to 5 p.m., was founded in 1893 and transferred hither in 1903. It contains valuable archaeological, anthropological and ethnological collections.

Our car speeds on through Rua Bartolomeu Dias, turns down Travessa da Saúde, crosses the railway line, passes in front of the Bom Sucesso Fort, and leaves near the *Torre de Belém*. This is indubitably one of the finest monuments in Lisbon and one of the most expressive memories of Portuguese military and naval power. (*See photo opposite*). This marvel of oriental architecture was erected in the Praia do Restello, famous as the point from which the ships sailed forth for the Great Discoveries, and was meant for the defence of the river and of the Portuguese capital. It was King Manuel I who ordered its erection; its was built within the river, and the project is due to the great master of "laced" architecture, Francisco de Arruda. It was begun in 1515 and completed six years afterwards. Later the river sank away from that point, leaving the Tower definitely connected with the shore. There died Dom Pedro da Cunha, father of Dom Rodrigo da Cunha, bishop of Porto; he was imprisoned there owing to his defence of the Prior of Crato, pretender to the throne during the first years of the Spanish dominion. There also were imprisoned several of the higher noblemen of the realm.

The Tower of Belém, seen from the outside, is a magnificent stone jewel, and it is with astonishment

Torre de Belem - Lado Sul.

and a growing appreciation that the stranger beholds its peculiar beauty. It is lace, and fine lace at that, in its delicate stonework which glimmers white afar, striking at once the sight of those on board ships entering the river. It is no less beautiful inside; and from its balconies and terraces there is a view of the river and of the sea beyond, which is not easily forgotten.

Crossing the drawbridge, we find ourselves in the first floor of the bridge, which is designed for the guns. Some gratings give us an idea of what the prison-cells must be like, to which those scant openings give a doubtful light. There are five of these underground cells, which no one has entered for a long time; they are reached by a stone stairway with 35 steps. Before they were used as cells, these rooms were used as powder magazines.

On the second floor used to be the Armoury and the Offices; on the third the Royal Room (Sala Regia—*see photo above*), with a magnificent balcony with columns of wonderful design; on the fourth the Refectory, outside which may be seen, in the floor, the holes through which molten lead should be cast in the case of assault to the fort; on the fifth was the Court, and it was here that a short while ago a commemorative stone was placed

LISBOA — Torre de Belem, Sala Régia

recording the great Lisbon–Rio de Janeiro air-raid*, in 1922, by Gago Coutinho and Sacadura Cabral. There is a sixth floor, which is the terrace, reached after going up 123 steps, and the view from which may be imagined.

We now begin to return. We follow the river bank, pass the dock where the Naval Aviation Centre is installed, and a few moments after passing in front of Jerónimos, find ourselves in *Praça Afonso de Albuquerque,* an ample space, with gardens, in the middle of which stands the monument to that great historic figure, the greatest of viceroys of India and the founder of modern imperialism. The monument was built with the legacy left by the historian Luz Soriano; it is in Manueline style and very high. The base contains four bas-reliefs representing the Defeat of the Moors in Malacca, the Reception of the Ambassador of the Kings of Narcinga, the Answer of Albuquerque to an offer of money, and the Delivery of the Keys of Goa, and four high reliefs with caravels and

This is an error on Pessoa's part. The two pilots mentioned were the first to fly from Lisbon to Rio de Janeiro, in 1922. No bombs were dropped . . .

62

galleons and other figures. On the top of the high column stands the statue, in bronze, of the great Viceroy. The statue was cast in the Army Arsenal. The monument is due to the architect Silva Pinto and the sculptor Costa Motta, and was unveiled in 1902.

It was at this point of the riverside that, in 1759, the noble family of Tavora was tortured and executed, with all others supposed to be concerned in the plot against King José's life.

On the left side of Praça Afonso de Albuquerque, the way we are going, stands the *Palácio Real de Belém (Royal Palace of Belém),* now the official residence of the President of the Republic. It was once inhabited by Queen Maria II, and afterwards by King Carlos, when still Crown Prince, after his marriage with Dona Amelia de Orleans. Some heads of foreign states stayed here when the guests of Portugal—King Edward VII, King Alfonso XIII, the Kaiser William II, Presidents Loubet, of France, and Hermes da Fonseca, of Brazil (the latter exactly on the occasion when the Republic was proclaimed in Portugal), as also Princes of Asturias and Amadeus of Savoy, the Counts of Paris, the Count d'Eu, the Dukes of Orléans, and many other members of foreign courts.

This building contains luxuriously furnished rooms, with fine paintings by Columbano, Malhoa, Leandro Braga, João Vaz, etc., and has a well-kept garden at the back. The Colonial Gardens *(Jardim Colonial)* are within its enclosure, and in the south part of the palace is the *Museu dos Coches* (Coach Museum), a very curious museum created in 1905 by the initiative of Queen Amelia. It contains 62 artistic vehicles, uniforms and liveries of the Royal House, uniforms of the crew of the royal boats, harnesses, stirrups, spurs, buttons, prints, portraits, etc. It is superior to its kindred museums at Versailles and

Madrid and has magnificent specimens of Portuguese seventeenth and eighteenth century art in such respects as the nature of the exhibits can show. Some of the vehicles are put away, and will only be exhibited when space for them is made by the building of the new gallery. The actual exhibits are as follows:

In the vestibule: the chariot of Senhora do Cabo (Our Lady of the Cape), used for the carrying of the image in the procession to Cape Espichel, with silver lanterns and torch-holders; three litters, in the Louis XV and XVI styles, with fine paintings; an *estafermo,* a wood and iron contrivance, shaped like a human being, with a shield and a long whip. This contrivance was used in tourneys to determine the swiftness of the horse and the horseman's skill. The vestibule also contains dards, lances, shields, harness and saddle-cloths.

In the hall, which measures 47 by 14 metres, was decorated by Francisco de Setúbal and other artists, and contains paintings depicting Science, Commerce, Abundance, Peace, Victory, Chivalry, Architecture, Painting, Sculpture, Music and mythological subjects, the following vehicles are exhibited: the coach of Philip II of Spain, a rare late sixteenth century specimen, which this king brought over to Portugal on his first visit; the coach of Dona Maria de Saboia, with fine paintings of the Louis XIV era; a coach of the later seventeenth century, a magnificent specimen of decoration; the coach of Dona Maria Anna de Austria, offered by Joseph I, Emperor of Austria, to his sister Maria Anna, bride of King João; the Crown Coach, so called because it has the royal emblem, which was ordered by King Pedro II for the marriage of Dom João; the coach of King João V, due to the architect Vicente Felix de Almeida and the sculptor José de Almeida, with valuable decorative work in carving and painting; the coach of Pope Clement XI, offered in 1715 by that Pontiff to Dom José; the coach of Prince Francisco, said to have been built in 1722; the coach of Dona Maria Anna Victoria, or Gold Column Coach; the coach of the Children of Palhava, who were the illegitimate sons of King João V; the coach of the embassy to Pope Clement XI, of wonderful and bold design, built in Rome; three magnificent specimens of artistic vehicles, with valuable carving; the coach of Dom José, remarkable for the woodwork; three chariots of the later eighteenth century, with graceful carving and painting; the coach of Dona Maria Benedicta, a sumptuous carriage used by Prince José's wife; the coach of Queen Maria, built for the solemnities of the dedication of the Basilica do Coração de Jesus, in Lisbon; three coaches of Queen Carlota Joaquina, sent over from Spain in 1785, a wedding gift of Carlos IV to his daughter; the Crown Carriage, built in England in 1826 for King João VI; five light carriages of the eighteenth century, and two chaises of the same period.

After examining all these larger exhibits, which give a quite vivid idea of the sumptuous court-life of Portugal in those periods, we ought to visit the showcases in the upper-floor galleries, where the exhibits of minor size are gathered together. There is a catalogue of the Museum by its Administrator, Luciano Freire. Admission is free, the Museum being open every day, except Friday, from 12.30 to 4.30 p.m. With special permission it may be visited before the regulation hours.

Our car now carries us swiftly on towards the Museum of Old Art *(Museu de Arte Antiga)*. On the way we shall pass the Overseas Barracks *(Quartel do Ultramar)* on our right and the Colonial Hospital on our left; further on, after the Santo Amaro electric car-barn, the Naval Barracks, the Jardim das Albertas (better known as da Rocha do Conde de Óbidos, under which style we have already alluded to it); and then we come to the *Museu de Arte Antiga,* which is installed in the old Palácio das Janellas Verdes (i.e., Green Window Palace), which was built in the seventeenth century for the Conde de Alvor.

This Museum, one of the finest in Lisbon, was founded in 1833 with objects that had belonged to the religious orders then dissolved, and other objects from the palace of Queen Carlota Joaquina. Several times added to, by various gifts and important purchases, it has come to be a repository of valuable works of art, especially since it came into the hands of its present Curator, Sr. José de Figueiredo, a well-known art-critic, and of a no less well-known art-master, sr. Luciano Freire. The Grupo de Amigos do Museu (Group of Friends of the Museum), recently constituted by the initiative of the Curator, has deserved very well of the Museum. The Library, organized there also by Sr. José de Figueiredo, contains already over 3,000 volumes covering the speciality.

The museum contains many and magnificent specimens of old masters of the several schools—Italian, Spanish, English, German, Flemish and Portuguese, and it has been recently enriched with some fine paintings which belonged to the great poet Guerra Junqueiro, a fine connoisseur.

If the collection of paintings is a fine one, the earthenware one is no less remarkable. It contains magnificent specimens of foreign and Portuguese work. The Oriental collection is most valuable, and includes Chinese, Japanese and Persian porcelains of extraordinary interest. There are fine specimens of Sèvres and Paris work, as also of English and German art. These installations are in the ground floor, which also contains fine Persian and Indian carpets, as also national carpets, from Arraiolos, Tavira, etc.

Right at the entrance we may see an enormous picture in glazed-tiles *(azulejos)* representing Lisbon in the seventeenth century, that is to say, as it was before the 1755 earthquake. In the vestibule there is a fine bas-relief figuring the *Descent from the Cross,* a sixteenth century work. We can see there also four Chinese eighteenth century jars, a Japanese one, and two Chinese vases.

Going up to the first floor, we find in the first room a show-case containing the celebrated Custódia dos Jerónimos, all in enamelled gold. The base, oval in shape, is divided into small pictures full of flowers and birds in enamelled high-relief; the lower frieze bears, in white enamelled lettering, the following inscription: *The Most High and Powerful King Dom Manuel I did have it made from the first gold of the Párias of Qilva. It was finished in CCCCCVI.* The "link" is formed by six spheres. The central body, between two pillars or groups of columns with several niches, in which are angels playing several instruments, sustains the hostiary, and, beneath it, the presentment of the twelve Apostles in adoration. The upper part, all in lace-work, shows in one space the image of God the Father, with the globe in His left hand, and giving the blessing with the right; the White Dove fills the lower space; and the whole is crowned by the Cross. This astonishing specimen of Portuguese gold-work was wrought in Lisbon by Gil Vicente by order of King Manuel I and following a sketch by Garcia de Resende. The weight of the gold is about 30 marks, and, as the inscription shows, this piece was wrought from the first gold received as a tribute from the King of Qilva. It was left by King Manuel I, in his will, to the Monastery of Belém. This sixteenth century marvel is 83 centimetres high.

In the various rooms which we shall now go through may be seen great pictures by Cristóvão de Moraes, Vieira Lusitano, Cristóvão Lopes, Vieira Portuense, Jorge

Affonso, Domingos Sequeira, Domingos Barbosa, two by Murillo, and some by Dürer, Pereda, Zurbarán, Ribera, Frans Hals, Teniers, Cuyp, Shalken, Jan Sievens, Rubens, Holbein, Melzi, Luini, Luca Giordano, Tintoretto, Antonio Moro, Fra Carlo, Patini, and others.

We go on next to the gold-work room. This collection is temporarily installed where it is now, but it can show marvels of an exceptional artistic value. It is chiefly composed of ritual objects, from the extinct convents, and of many others in gold and silver, many of them adorned with precious stones, as for instance the *Relicário da Madre de Deus,* which is of enamelled gold set with pearls, emeralds and rubies. Other specimens, of remarkable value and beauty, are the noteworthy *Custódia de Frei João Dornellas,* in gilt silver, dating from the fourteenth century, the precious *Custódia da Bemposta,* 97 centimetres high, in gilt silver set with stones, the rock crystal crucifixes, and many other items which never fail to attract and engage the attention of the visitor.

There is the sketch room too, which contains much magnificent work, both national and foreign, the remarkable work of Domingos Sequeira figuring there. The Museum is open every day, except Monday, from 11 a.m. to 5 p.m. Admission is of course free.

We shall now go along Rua das Janellas Verdes, near the end of which, on the left, stands a big old building which was once the Convento dos Marianos. In one of the outhouses of this building there is a modern printing office, the *Imprensa Ltda.,* where this work is set up and printed.

We go up Rua de Santos-o-Velho, pass the French Legation, in Calçada do Marquês de Abrantes, and then up the Avenida Wilson (formerly Avenida das Cortes) at the top of which stands the Palace of the Congress of the Republic; this was once the Convent of São Bento da Saúde, the adaptation to its present use, which entailed great modifications, being due to the architect Ventura Terra. The Chamber of Deputies, decorated by the sculptor Teixeira Lopes, is a vast amphitheatre, with a metal dome, full of light and with fair acoustic conditions. The Senate, an amphitheatre also, is smaller but equally harmonious as a whole. The Sala dos Passos Perdidos has decorations by Columbano, Ceia and João Vaz.

In the right wing of the building are the National Archives, called Torre do Tombo, installed there since 1757. The archives are remarkable for the enormous collection of documents they contain; there may all the past life of Portugal and of its people be investigated and studied. There are to be found historic books in rare copies, often of incalculable value, diplomatic documents of great importance and interest, and a veritable museum of printed, and manuscript rarities related to many of the chief facts in the history of Portugal, from the very beginnings of its life as an independent nation. A great number of volumes illuminated by specialists in this art will also be found in the Torre do Tombo.

Having now effected this short but interesting visit to Lisbon, and having seen all that is most interesting, or, at least, is most likely to interest the tourist, especially if art and beauty appeal to him, it is natural that we should now return to the hotel, which, as we have said, will most likely be one in the very centre of the city.

Evening amusements are not lacking, for there are first-class theatres and other similar pastimes, but, to make the best of this stay, let us carry the tourist to the building where the Clube dos Restauradores (Maxim's) is installed. This building is the old Palácio Foz, built in the seventeenth century on the plan laid down by the Italian architect Fabri; this palace belonged first to the Marquises of Castello Melhor, but it was bought later by the Marquis da Foz, who modified it within in 1870–1875 with the aid of excellent artists whose work he himself supervised. We find there, indeed, fine work due to the architect Gaspar, to the sculptor Leandro Braga, to the painter Francisco Villaça, and, above all, to the master-painter Columbano Bordalo Pinheiro; there are also fine paintings by foreign artists of renown.

The entrance is through an ample vestibule, sober and full of dignity, which contains fine canvases by the Italian Manini, a fine marble figure of a woman on a shell, and a Greek bas-relief, in white marble framed in black marble. Thence rises the fine staircase in Italian marble, sumptuous and neat, which leads to the gallery which surrounds it at the top and the columns of which are also in the same magnificent stone. The handrail of the staircase, richly decorated in copper and steel, opens with a sheep's head in shining copper. Other decorative motives follow, with the crest of the noble family of the Marquises da Foz. This admirable work—the handrail—was executed in Paris and cost then no less than £ 9,000. It is a more sumptuous specimen than that of the Chateau de Chantilly, of the Dukes d'Aumale, which is held to be the most beautiful one in the world. The columns of the gallery rise from marble pedestals, and the base and top are of copper. The upper gallery contains two fine canvases by Snijders, *The Fruit Seller* and *The Fish Seller,* one by Bruyère, *The Triumph of Louis XIV,* and the arms of the Foz family by Francisco Villaya.

The first hall, all in oak, has a fine fireplace in coloured marble crowned by two wooden caryatids, sculptured by Jean Goujon; these, executed with an extreme lightness of touch, seem to sustain the ceiling, which is decorated with a painting of the French School. The ballroom is worth seeing, for the style of its decorations, a fine work due to Leandro Braga, whose hand is seen in several other details of the palace. This room was designed on the lines of one in the Palace of Queluz; the ceiling shows a painting by Venix, representing the Birth of Venus. Other paintings in the ceiling are by Columbano. One thing to be noticed is the wealth of the crystal chandeliers which light the several rooms of this building.

This palace was bought several years ago by the Conde de Sucena, and the United States Legation was installed there for a long time. The Club dos Restauradores, or Maxim's, is now in occupation, and its management has scrupled in preserving carefully all the original decorative elements. This leads many tourists to visit this Club as the most comfortable and sumptuous in Lisbon. As it is situated right in the centre of the city, at the very beginning of Avenida da Liberdade, it is naturally the place of the kind most indicated for a visit. The Club has a splendid and ample dining-room, where, in the evenings, artistes of various kinds, and manifold attractions, are to be found. It is considered the first establishment of its sort in the country. A radio reception post has been installed.

We do not wish to be over-lengthy in these descriptions. But, acting on the supposition that the tourist can stay one day more, we shall proceed to indicate a small tour he can make within the city; in the course of it he will have occasion to see a few interesting things.

Taking a motor-car in the Rossio, we go up the Chiado and find ourselves in Praça Luís de Camões, where stands the statue to the great national poet, to which (see p.40) we have already alluded. We then enter Rua do Loreto and will shortly find, on our right, the palatial building belonging to the Dukes of Palmela, which was once inhabited by them and now contains the *Centro Nacional de Esgrima,* the *Automóvel Club de Portugal,* the *Aero Club,* the *Liga Naval Portuguesa* and the *Museu Nacional da Marinha,* which represents the product of several years work of the late King Carlos, in his favourite oceanographical explorations. This museum contains fishes, molluscs and crustacea of the Portuguese coasts, specimens drawn from several depths and several distances, as also sea-birds of our fauna, and the *odontespisnosutus,* a hitherto unknown animal. There will also be found pictures with drawings of remarkable specimens, photos of work on board during these explorations, diagrams of soundings, apparatus used in them, a library, King Carlos' diplomas, obtained by him in several exhibitions, a log-book, etc. This Museum, which was installed with the permission of King Manuel II, with furniture taken from the Royal Palace, is open to the public from 11 a.m. to 4 p.m. on all days, which are not holidays.

Just beyond this building lies the one containing the *Caixa Geral de Depósitos,* installed there in 1887. It was in this palace that Wellington and Beresford had their headquarters from 1811 to 1813. Nearly in front stands the Azambuja palace where the offices of a newspaper, *A Lucta,* were once installed; a political club now occupies the place.

Going down Rua Marechal Saldanha, which lies on our left, we are brought to the so called *Alto de Santa Catarina,* a high place which commands a view of the Tagus in its greatest breadth as well as the land on the South bank of the river. This is one of the best places for a view of the river; it is here that crowds gather whenever they wish to see a particularly fine fleet enter the Tagus, or on those nights when there are commemorative fireworks out in the river.

Coming back now, and following the route we were originally taking, down Calçada do Combro, we find on our right a huge old building where the General Post Office once stood; it has now been for many years the location of the *Confederação Geral do Trabalho,* of other trade unions, and of the workmen's journal *A Batalha.* It is amusing to note that in the very same building, though on the side facing the back street, is located the *Juventudes Monárquicas,* one of the chief royalist organisations.

We now turn off into Rua do Século. Right at the beginning, at the first corner, there is the *Capela das Mercês,* the chapel where, on the 6th June 1699, the future Marquis de Pombal, then given the name of Sebastião José de Carvalho e Melo, was baptised. It was there that the tomb containing his bones stood, till they were transferred to the Igreja da Memória (see p.54).

Further on, on our left, stands the large building of the newspaper *O Século.* This is the only Portuguese paper which had a building made expressly for it. The installation is, as may be supposed, ample and full of light. In the vast basement, served by lifts, are the large printing machines, on the ground floor the management—an admirably installed office, by the way—on the first floor the editorial, and on the second the type-setting department. In the primitive part of the building, which once belonged to the Viscount da Lançada, are the Editor's office, the archives, and the exhibition and concert halls. The *Século* is one of the largest Portuguese papers, with a very wide circulation and very carefully informed; it is a present conservative in politics. Its proprietors publish other things—books, weeklies, etc.—and the printing department also works for outsiders.

In front of this building lies the *Calçada dos Caetanos,* where stands the building of the *Conservatório Nacional de*

Música, founded in 1836 by Almeida Garrett, and lately quite rebuilt. We have now entered the so-called *Bairro Alto* (High Quarter), where the majority of Lisbon papers have their offices.

Returning to Rua do Século, we see, next to that paper's building, the semi-palatial residence where, on the 13th May 1699, the Marquis de Pombal was born; a commemorative stone was placed there in 1923. The Spanish Consulate and Chamber of Commerce now occupy this building.

Turning the corner into the old Rua do Arco a Jesus— so-called from the arch *(arco)* which is still there—, our car will pass by the *Academia das Ciências de Lisboa,* from which the street draws its present name. This building was once the seat of the Convento de Jesus; and at present, besides the Academy, it contains the Faculty of Letters and the Geological Museum.

The *Academia das Ciências de Lisboa,* founded in 1779, has its seat here since 1834 and owns a remarkable library, located in a large room, 31 metres long, 15 wide and 11 high, which is one of the finest halls of its kind in all Europe. The library includes 116,000 volumes printed since 1500, 112 incunabula and 1,600 manuscripts. Part of the contents was bought by the Academy, and part once belonged to the library of the old Convent, of the Third Franciscan Order (of Penitence, as it was called), which had its seat there since 1582. The library extends beyond the large hall at which we have alluded; it occupies twelve other rooms. There are many rare works in this collection, as, for instance, the 1610 *Missal,* a manuscript illuminated by Estêvão Gonçalves, which used to serve to take the oath of the Portuguese Kings on their accession; a Latin Bible, First Edition, printed in parchment in Mainz in 1462 by Gutenberg's partners (the copy is in an admirable state), this and the copy in the National Library being the only two extant in Portugal; a Hebrew *Pentateuch,* printed in Lisbon in 1491, a remarkable specimen of national printing; a collection of Arabic MSS; a copy of the first edition (1572) of *The Lusiads* of Camões, etc.

The 34 busts which decorate the cornice, made by the Real Fabrica de Louça do Rato, represent King Joao VI, several saints and prelates, philosophers (e.g., Plato), mathematicians (e.g., Pedro Nunes and Newton), scientists (e.g., Hippocrates and Verney), orators (e.g., Cicero), poets (e.g., Virgil, Sá de Miranda and Camões), chronicle-writers (e.g., Damião de Góis and João de Barros), etc.

The Academia das Ciéncias has a museum of its own, which contains antiquities, coins, medals, specimens of old earthenware, etc.

On the second floor is the *Geological Museum,* which is held to be one of the best of its kind in all Europe. There are six rooms, containing all sorts of exhibits of the speciality fossils, human and animal skulls and bones, silex implements, primitive earthenware and sculpture work, and a special library. This Museum is open on weekdays from 10.30 a.m. to 5 p.m.

There is another tour the visitor can effect, if he wishes to devote the afternoon to it. Our car leaves the Rossio in a different direction, going up Rua da Palma. In this route we have on our right the mass of houses constituting the quarter called the *Mouraria,* a popular quarter, like Alfama, and as distinctive and characteristic as this is.

A little further on, almost in front of the Apollo Theatre, we take Rua 20 de Abril, better known by its former name of Rua de São Lazaro, and, in so doing, we shall leave on our left, in crossing Largo do Socorro, Rua

José Antonio Serrano, which leads to *Hospital de São José (St. Joseph's Hospital)*. This Hospital is the largest in Lisbon and dates back to 1775. The building formerly belonged to the Jesuits, and was their Convento de Santo Antão-o-Novo, built by Dom Henrique. The Hospital has fine glazed-work in the vestibule and a chapel with good marble. Going right up this way, we get to the *Campo dos Mártires da Pátria,* so called in memory of the executions which took place there in 1817 of the conspirators, led by Gomes Freire, against the British governor Beresford. This space once contained a wooden bullring, which was pulled down as soon as the Campo Pequeno Ring was thought of. There was once a chapel to St. Anna here; hence the name of Campo de Santa Anna, by which this place was, and to a certain extent still is, known.

One of the sides of this large square, which contains a very well kept garden, is occupied by the building of the Faculty of Medicine, which is faced by the monument (by Costa Motta, unveiled in 1907) to a great Portuguese physician, *Sousa Martins.*

The Building of the *Faculty of Medicine,* designed by engineer Cabral Couceiro and architect José Maria Nepomuceno, with modifications by engineers Borges de Castro and Abecassis and architect Leonel Gaia, dates only from 1911. It has a fine main stairway, a central vestibule with galleries, with plates containing the names of professors of the School, and a bust of Dr. Manuel Bento de Sousa, by Teixeira Lopes, unveiled in 1904. The painter Columbano decorated the Council Hall, which also contains bronze busts. In the vestibule there are paintings by Antonio Ramalho and a statue of Medicine by Costa Motta. On the first floor there is a hall with paintings by Joao Vaz and glazed-work by Jorge Collaço. The Examination Hall has friezes by Velloso Salgado, a ceiling by João Vaz and a portrait painted by Malhoa.

The Faculty of Medicine, formerly Lisbon Medical School, was located in St. Joseph's Hospital till 1910; it was only after its transference to the new building that it constituted the Faculty of Medicine, properly so called.

On the right hand side of the Faculty of Medicine is Rua do Instituto Bacteriológico, where this institute, which takes its name from Dr. Câmara Pestana, is located since 1892, when it was founded. The building originally belonged to the old Convento de Santa Anna, was adapted to its present purpose by Dr. Câmara Pestana, a great bacteriologist, who died a martyr of science owing to his work during the bubonic plague epidemic in Oporto in 1899. At the corner of this street and of Travessa do Thorel there still stands: part of the original Convent; it is now occupied by the Asilo de Santa Anna, which belongs to the Sociedade da Infância Desvalida—an orphans' home.

On the left of the Medical School, in Rua Manuel Bento de Sousa, lie the *Instituto de Medicina Legal* and the Mortuary *(Morgue)*. From the grating of this garden a fine view may be had of that high part of the city that lies East. In the Campo itself there also stands the present residence of the Cardinal Patriarch of Lisbon, offered him by the Catholics of Portugal.

To get to the point of the city we have been describing there are other routes besides the one we took. We can come up the Calçada de Santa Anna which leads up to the Rua do Instituto Bacteriológico; we can come up straight from the Avenida by the Lavra Elevator; we can go round by Rua das Pretas and up Rua de Santo António dos Capuchos; or we can simply take the Gomes Freire tram.

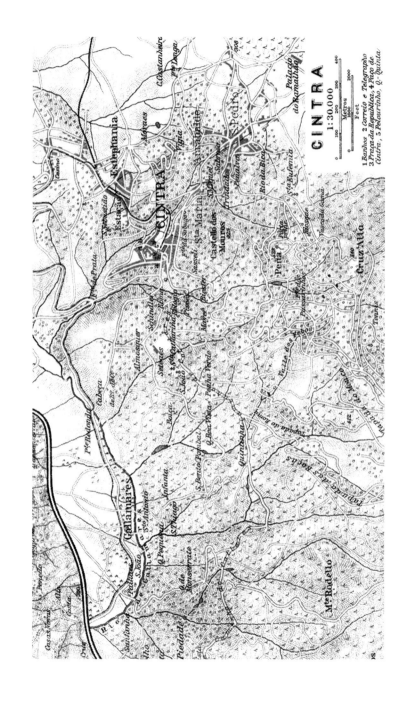

CINTRA

1:30.000

Metres

Feet

1 Banhos 2 Correio e Telegrapho
3 Praça da Republica, 4 Paço de
Cintra, 5 Pelourinho, Qª Quinta

A Visit to Cintra, via Queluz

The tourist who is visiting Portugal should not limit his sight-seeing to the capital, though he will find in it, as we have shown, many and many things to evoke both his artistic and his historic sense. Anyone new to Lisbon is at once struck by the unparalleled beauty of the Tagus basin, of the views that may be had from the top of its seven hills, of its gardens and monuments, of its old streets and latest arteries. But the suburbs are worth seeing for themselves. They also are full of beauties—not only natural, for the landscape is admirable round Lisbon, but also historical, for a great number of buildings to be seen there are strongly evocative of the past.

We shall therefore now move out towards the suburbs of Lisbon, and we are sure that the tourist that goes with us will not think any minute lost of the time he spends with us on this little tour.

Our car leaves Rossio, goes up Avenida da Liberdade, takes to the right and then to the left, up Avenida Antonio Augusto de Aguiar, leaves, on its left, the Spanish Legation (a typical old palatial building) and passes, a little further on, and on the same side, the Palhava Sports Ground, till it reaches the *Jardim Zoológico* (Zoological Gardens), one of the most pleasant places just outside Lisbon, and much sought by the population on holidays. These Gardens have an area of 92.540 square metres and contain animals from almost all parts of the world. The Zoological Gardens were established in 1884, though not where they now stand; they used to be further down, nearer the city, in a large park situated in the crossing of Avenida António Augusto de Aguiar and Estrada de Bemfica, which is the road we enter when we leave the former avenue. It was afterwards transferred to the large grounds where it is now situated.

Entrance-fee to this splendid park costs 2.50 escudos on Thursdays (a special day there) and 2.00 escudos on other days. In the ticket office they supply a plan giving the exact distribution of all cages and places, so nothing may be left unseen. On Thursdays and Sundays there is a *thé dansant* there.

Somewhat further on, still going up Estrada de Bemfica, we find, on our right, Rua Duarte Galvão, which leads to the Bemfica Sanatorium; then, on our left, the long wall, just like that of a castle, which limits the palace and park which used to belong to Dr. Carvalho Monteiro. Our car now enters Travessa de S. Domingos de Bemfica, and, leaving on its left the property of Visconde Silva Carvalho, crosses the railway line and passes by the old *Convento de S. Domingos de Bemfica*, where, in its earlier times, the Royal Palace of Bemfica stood. King João I made a gift of it to the Order of St. Dominic (S. Domingos), which founded the convent. It is at present occupied by the one of the two sections of the Pupillos do Exército (Army Pupils) School. In the convent church, wrecked by the 1755 earthquake, and afterwards rebuilt, there is fine glazed work and some remarkable tombs, including that of the great lawyer João das Regras. Next to the convent stands the *Quinta da Infanta Dona Isabel*, a property which once belonged to this princess, daughter of King João VI. It is now a reformatory. In front of this, on an eminence, stands the Palace of the *Marquises da Fronteira*, an old building, remarkable in architecture, admirably designed and decorated; many important points in Portuguese military and literary history are connected with it. On the left side of this palace there are gardens which are an artistic marvel; on the right there is a road going to Serra de Monsanto. This fine property, now belonging to D. José de Mascarenhas the younger, a descendant of the

Marquises, may be visited by obtaining permission in the palace itself.

Returning to Estrada de Bemfica, up which a tramline runs, we now soon reach the end of this line. This is *Bemfica* proper, a recent, but populous, quarter of the city, which is still suburb enough to be much visited on Sundays and on summer evenings. On the left, going uphill, is *Parque Silva Porto,* a popular holiday place.

During all this route, we have constantly had Serra de Monsanto in view on our left.

Our car moves on now, definitely out of the city (for the city itself reaches as far as Bemfica), and it soon comes to the fine village of *Amadora,* 13 kms outside Lisbon. The development of this suburb is quite recent, and it has many nice modern houses. There is an aviation ground there.

Further on, 15 kms from Lisbon, is *Queluz;* and it must be noted that all these places—Bemfica itself, Amadora and Queluz—are on the railway line from Lisbon to Cintra, which latter place are now steadily approaching.

Queluz is remarkable for its Royal Palace, built in parts, from 1758 to 1794. This is one of the most curious buildings of the time—sumptuous, noble, with fine gardens and a historic past that surrounds it with interest. It began, as a matter of fact, as a mere country house belonging to the Marquês de Castelo Rodrigo; it became afterwards, by confiscation, national property. It was the scene of several scandalous passages of royal lives; and the building, successively added to and bettered finally reached the degree of magnificence which, in its general lines, it still maintains. Besides having been the residence of kings and princes, it was used by Junot as his dwelling during the French invasion of Portugal; and Junot himself had some part in altering and adding to the building.

The palace contains various rooms with special names—the Sala da Tocha (Torch-Room), Sala dos Archeiros (Archers Room), Sala dos Bilhares (Billiard-Room), Sala dos Particulares, Sala dos Embaixadores (Ambassadors' Room), the best in the palace and finely decorated with paintings and inlaid work; the Sala das Açafatas; the Sala do Toucador da Rainha, with fine paintings, and once Dom Miguel's bedroom; the bedroom of Queen Carlota Joaquina; the Oratory; the Sala de D. Quixote (Don Quixote Room), with canvases representing several phases in the novel hero's life (this room was the bedroom of King Pedro III and Queen Maria I, as also of other royal persons, and it contains a wax bust of King João VI); the Sala das Merendas, the Dining, Coffee, Smoking, Sculpture and Lanternet (Lanternim) Rooms, the Music and Throne Rooms, and so on. All these rooms are rich decorated and have fine mirrors.

The park is one of the finest in Portuguese royal buildings. It is made up of three distinct gardens—the Neptune Garden, the Azereiros Gardens, and the Park properly such. The park contains many species of trees and plants, ponds and statues, and glazed work showing the court life in the bridge over the little stream which crosses the gardens.

Very near Queluz (one km off) is the village of *Belas* (14 kms from Lisbon), where there is a splendid property, once belonging the Marquises of Belas; this was one time the residence of King Duarte, and afterwards of Dona Brites, mother of King Manuel I. It now belongs to Sr. Borges de Almeida. On the other side of this village lie several other picturesque ones, with beautiful pine-woods, and properties like the *Quinta do Bomjardim,* which once belonged to the Conde de Redondo and now belongs to the Marquis de Borba. All this region is remarkable for its fine air and magnificent water.

On going out of Queluz, we pass under one of the arches of the Aqueduct which carries water to Lisbon; and a little further on, where the road begins its descent towards Cacém, we catch sight of the Serra de Cintra (Cintra Hill) in all its splendour, the side more visible to us being that which bears the Castle of the Moors.

We next pass Cacém (18 kms from Lisbon) which is a railway junction. It is to the point to mention, at this stage of our narrative, that the small voyage we have been making on a motor-car can likewise be effected by rail. The Companhia dos Caminhos de Ferro Portugueses (see p.18) has a fine railway service, at short intervals, between Lisbon and Cintra, taking in all the chief villages in between. At Cacém the railway line branches out, one branch going to Cintra, the other towards *Caldas da Rainha* (109 kms from Lisbon) and *Figueira da Foz* (220 kms from Lisbon), two health and pleasure resorts which are very popular throughout the country and in Spain.

A few minutes more and Cintra itself (28 kms from Lisbon) appears, girt sometimes in a thin veil of mist, bathed, at other times, in a great splendour of sunlight.

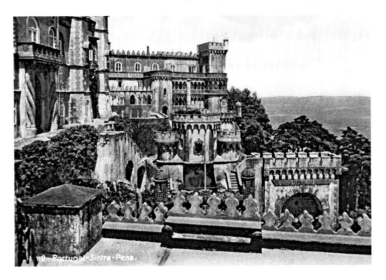

Lightning Source UK Ltd.
Milton Keynes UK
UKOW04f1843160115

244638UK00001B/73/P